NAPOLEON'S
EVERYDAY
GOURMET
PLANK GRILLING

NAPOLEON'S
EVERYDAY GOURMET PLANK GRILLING

INSPIRED RECIPES BY CHEF **TED READER**

KEY PORTER BOOKS

Library and Archives Canada Cataloguing in Publication

Reader, Ted
    Napoleon's everyday gourmet plank grilling: inspired recipes / by Ted Reader.

ISBN 978-1-55470-272-5

    1. Plank cookery. 2. Barbecue cookery.
I. Napoleon Appliance Corporation II. Title. III. Title: Everyday gourmet plank grilling.

TX840.B3R4248 2010   641.5'784   C2009-905119-2

ONTARIO ARTS COUNCIL
CONSEIL DES ARTS DE L'ONTARIO

The publisher gratefully acknowledges the support of the Canada Council for the Arts and the Ontario Arts Council for its publishing program. We acknowledge the support of the Government of Ontario through the Ontario Media Development Corporation's Ontario Book Initiative.

We acknowledge the financial support of the Government of Canada through the Book Publishing Industry Development Program (BPIDP) for our publishing activities.

Key Porter Books Limited
Six Adelaide Street East, Tenth Floor
Toronto, Ontario
Canada M5C 1H6

www.keyporter.com

Design: Martin Gould
Electronic formatting: Jean Lightfoot Peters
Photography: Mike McColl

Printed and bound in Canada

10 11 12 13 14 6 5 4 3 2 1

As the largest family-owned hearth and grill manufacturer in North America, Napoleon maintains strong family values that carry through in every aspect of the organization. Since 1976, Napoleon has grown from a small manufacturing operation to a large private corporation instilling the same solid values that it began with. Napoleon products are found in homes around the globe and have become the preferred brand choice worldwide.

TABLE OF CONTENTS

This book is dedicated to our loyal Napoleon owners across the world who have entrusted us with their home comfort needs, and to our family of associates at the Napoleon group of companies. None of this would be possible without you.

NAPOLEON APPLIANCE CORPORATION

To the sweetness of my kids Layla and Jordan.
You are the greatest joy in my life.
You bring happiness, smiles, kisses and, above all, the truth about life.

THANK YOU
LOVE, DADDY

FOREWORD

Our first foray at a hardcover cookbook with Ted Reader was an eye-opening experience in both the creativity and long, exhausting hours of work involved. The positive feedback we received from both loyal Napoleon owners and readers new to the brand inspired us to jump into our second book and push the limits of the grilling world with a book strictly dedicated to planking and cooking with natural wood. You'll find mouth-watering photos and easy-to-follow instructions to make your grilling world come alive with the smell of traditionally smoked food, the untraditional way. Enjoy.

THE SCHROETER FAMILY

ACKNOWLEDGEMENTS

First and foremost, thanks to Ted Reader and his talented ensemble of grilling gurus who push the envelope and make us stretch the limits of our imagination in the epicurean world of grilling. The fine staff at Key Porter Books with their undying support and, of course, everyone at Napoleon Appliance Corporation who throw their heart and soul into every Napoleon grill.

THE SCHROETER FAMILY

My Wife Pamela: Pamela my love, mother of my two beautiful children, thank you for all your support in life and in my career. You are my rock. You have stood by me through all the fire and smoke. From over 100 grills in the yard to the complete invasion and culinary chaos in your world; thank you for keeping me motivated, encouraged and loved. You are my inspiration!

The Schroeter Family: Ingrid, Wolfgang, Christopher and Stephen, thank you for all your support and encouragement over the past years. Your grills are the best, they make my food sing.

Napoleon Appliance Corporation: Thank you to all those involved at Napoleon in creating the best grills in the world. Your support and dedication to me is greatly appreciated.
napoleongrills.com

David Coulson: Thanks for your continued support over the years. You are a grilling inspiration and a warrior around the horseshoe pit!

Greg Cosway and Les Murray: My business partners and most importantly my friends. Thank you for all your support, guidance and encouragement. Thanks for the direction in helping me find the drive to move things forward. Here is to all the delicious smoke and fire we create.
tedreader.com

Caiti McLelland and Erin Pierce: "The girls in the office"—we all know you girls are the glue, thanks for holding it all together ladies.
eventrix.ca

Key Porter Books: Jordan and the gang at Key Porter thank you for your support. Your belief in Ted Reader is awesome. Much love guys.
keyporter.com

Dana McCauley and Associates: Thank you for your support in helping me get this book finished. Sabrina's editing and writing skills truly made this book easy and fun to write.
danamccauley.com

Mike McColl: Mike thank you for all your hard work on this cookbook. Your photos are edible. Congratulations on capturing my food. You have been a great asset to my business, not only as my chef but as well as my friend.
generalchefery.com

Mia Bachmaier: Principal Food Stylist—Thank you for all your hard work on this cookbook. Your artistry with the food styling makes my recipes look magically delicious.

Geoffrey, Daniel and Peter—Thanks for your hard work and new found friendships. Geoffrey you are a gastronomic marvel—Cheers lads!
enville.com

Bryn Clarke: Chef's Assistant—Thanks for your hard work and dedication.

Ralph James: Agent of the year! You got it going and then kept it moving—Thanks man!
theagencygroup.com

Sleeman Brewery: Delicious beer with time honored tradition based on family recipes—John you make good beer!
sleeman.com

Brown-Forman: Southern Comfort, Jack Daniel's, Gentleman Jack, Finlandia Vodka, Chambord and El Jimador Tequila—Thanks for keeping it real Ross—Real fun!
brown-forman.com

Lindemans Wines: Awesome Tasty Treats from Down Under. Perfect wines matched for plank grilling.
lindemans.com

Metro Grocery Stores: Gillian Kerr and Lori Falvo thanks for your ongoing support. For *Food at its best*—Shop Metro!
metro.ca

Honeyman's Beef Purveyors: Will Wallace thanks for all the great meats—Beef, Pork, Chicken and Turkey—Yummy!
honeymansbeef.com

Top Meadow Farms: Artisan beef, tender and delicious.
topmeadowfarms.com

Heritage Salmon: Adam Kennedy a long time supporter. Thanks for the salmon, fresh cod and trout. Delicious!
cookaqua.com

Stephen Murdoch: You are the best Publicist a guy could ask for. Keep up the great work!

Graham Bauckham: Thank you for providing my bbq shelter.
varsitytents.com

TED READER CREDITS:

Chef Ted Reader: Author, Recipe Development, Writing, Editing, Food Styling, Prop Styling and BBQ Guru

Pamela Jacobson: Director of BBQ Operations, Ted Reader Inc.

Mike McColl: Photographer

Mia Bachmaier: Principal Food Stylist/Chef
Peter Gorka: Chef
Bryn Clarke: Chef's Assistant, Prep, Shopping

Greg Cosway: Manager

Les Murray: Business Manager

Ralph James: Agent

Blair Holder: Legal Counsel

—Ted Reader

INTRODUCTION

When we first started to contemplate our second cookbook's style and contents, it brought us back to the early days of Napoleon: Wood!

The company first started producing wood stoves in the depths of the oil crisis back in the 1970s to address the demand for an economical alternative to fossil-fuel-based heat. As fuel prices stabilized and consumers were looking for an easier and more convenient way to supplement home heating, Napoleon started to specialize in gas fireplaces. Producing two units initially, Napoleon now manufactures literally dozens of fireplace designs to match any decor and features many award-winning designs throughout the company's full complement of products, from fireplaces, inserts and stoves, to outdoor heaters, fireplaces, gas fire pits and water features, as well as a complete line of HVAC products.

In the 1990s Napoleon embraced outdoor living and decided to design and market a line of sophisticated gas grills. The thinking behind this bold move was that it would not only keep our associates busy year round, but would allow Napoleon to venture into a new, exciting market. Not being a company to rest on its laurels, the design engineers came up with a way to use charcoal *and* wood on its gas grills, coming full circle to where we started using wood exclusively in our products more than 30 years ago. And here we have it: the inspiration for a complete cookbook on grilling with wood planks. It is only fitting that the book specializes in what initially helped start the company so long ago.

This is not simply a book dedicated to "wood" or "charcoal" cooking, it's a masterpiece of ingenuity based on grilling with planks of wood. From appetizers, main course meals and desserts, you'll stretch your grilling prowess and absolutely amaze your family and friends with your very own planked delights.

PLANK EVOLUTION

Cooking on planks originated in the Pacific Northwest. It was a common practice of the Native Haida people of this region. The Haida would strap a whole salmon between two cedar boards, place it on the hot coals of a bonfire, and slow roast their meals.

For me, it all started back in the early 1990s. I had just started taping my television show, *Cottage Country*. During the first season of the show, I developed my cedar-planked salmon recipe. I was understandably nervous about planking for the first time on my new TV show. Thankfully, the salmon was delicious, the plank didn't catch fire, and the boathouse was still standing at the end of it!

I continued to learn and practice the art of planking and then I got my big break. I was developing recipes for the *President's Choice Barbecue Cookbook* at the time. My boss requested that we have an awesome salmon recipe for the book. It was the perfect opportunity to whip up my signature cedar-planked salmon. Everyone in the kitchen loved it. In fact, they loved it so much that it was the feature recipe of the entire book, which eventually sold approximately 150,000 copies. Loblaws customers even received a free cedar plank with the purchase of a pound of salmon. Cedar-planked salmon was a huge hit and is still one of my all-time favorite recipes.

In 1999 my friend Kathleen Sloan and I wrote *Sticks and Stones: The Art of Grilling on Plank, Vine and Stone*, the first book written on the subject. The book became a Canadian bestseller and won a silver medal at the 2000 Cuisine Canada Cookbook Awards. It is also on the suggested reading list for students at the Culinary Institute of America. Many plank grillers call it their planking bible. Even Steven Raichlen, famous BBQ guru in the U.S. and author of *BBQ USA* (Workman Publishing, 2003) called *Sticks and Stones* "an ingenious book."

It often amazes me how popular plank grilling has become over the past ten years. It's everywhere; books, magazines, celebrity chefs like Martha Stewart and Emeril Lagasse have joined me in cooking with planks. Plank grilling has even been embraced by restaurants such as The Keg Steakhouse, Baton Rouge and Seasons 52.

I have planked between 3,000 and 5,000 planks annually for the past eight years and I have more than a few new tricks, techniques, and recipes up my sleeve. Plank grilling is such an easy way to cook: there's no turning, flipping or fussy cleanup. Essentially planking is a hot, fast way to smoke foods without needing to own a smoker.

I couldn't have tested (and eaten) all of these recipes on my own. I work with amazing chefs who worked on this book just as hard as I did. My team of bandits is the backbone of this grilling and barbecuing machine.

This book includes recipes as well as insider's tips and techniques. The recipes range from easy to difficult, but they all have easy-to-follow step-by-step instructions and all of them are tasty. I love to plank and I've discovered that there is nothing that you can't plank. I plank because it's simple, it's fun, and the results are utterly delicious. I hope you have as much fun preparing these recipes as I did creating them.

**CHEERS,
TEDDY READER**

THE BASICS OF GREAT PLANK GRILLING

Here is your super-simple planking checklist:

SOAK 'EM
Soak all planks in cold water for a minimum of 1 hour. Weigh the plank down with something heavy to keep it submerged. For best flavor and smoke results, soak the plank for 4 hours.

SMOKE 'EM
Preheat grill to the appropriate temperature (thickness of the plank and type of food will dictate temperature) with the grill lid closed. Place the plank on the grill; close the lid and heat for 3 to 5 minutes or until plank begins to crackle and smoke.

FLAVOR 'EM
For added flavor, season the plank with coarse sea salt, cracked black pepper and/or fresh herbs.

Dos
- Soak plank
- Season plank
- Keep lid closed
- Be careful
- Have fun

Don'ts
- Leave grill unattended
- Flip food
- Flip plank
- Peek constantly
- Be careless

EAT 'EM UP
Carefully remove the hot plank from the grill using heavy-duty tongs and set on a presoaked, raw plank. Transfer the smoked, cooked food to serving plates or platters. Place the hot plank in a bucket of cold water to cool down. Dig in and eat 'em up!

THE GREAT DEBATE

GAS VS. CHARCOAL PLANKING

These recipes were tested using a variety of Napoleon gas grills, from the small portable FreeStyle™ grill all the way up to the PV infrared/gas/charcoal grill. A great all-purpose Napoleon grill is one of my Ted Reader Signature Series Grills. We also used the new Napoleon M605RBCSS Charcoal Grill to test some of the recipes. We particularly liked the Napoleon Gemini™ grill. And just for fun we used my personal Fire Pit el Fogo, a hardwood-fueled bonfire pit.

Whether you are using a gas or charcoal grill to cook food on planks, it needs to have a proper-fitting lid. This will keep the smoke near the food and ensure temperature consistency.

Charcoal or hardwood grills are best for flavor, but the award for best planking grill goes to natural gas or propane-fueled grills. Gas grills can maintain temperature consistently and offer excellent fuel control, two qualities crucial when plank grilling since most recipes require you to use a low and slow (that's low temperature and a long cooking time) method.

Charcoal grills reach about 750°F (399°C) when at their hottest, whereas most gas grills cap out at about 600°F (315°C). For fast, high-heat plank grilling, a charcoal grill is the way to go: big flavor, great heat, and fast cook times. A high heat thermometer in the grill lid is a must; so if your grill doesn't have one, place an oven thermometer inside the grill to keep tabs on the temperature. Low and slow recipes are great when cooked over the hot coals of an open fire pit; this method is not only rustic and authentic but also creates the best flavor.

Although each recipe and every grill is different, it's key that you achieve consistent heat to have good results. So, keep the lid closed as much as possible to maintain heat and smoke. Plank cooking doesn't necessarily need to be done on high heat. I used to get so psyched about extreme heat that I ignored the wonders of low and slow cooking. When you take your time with plank grilling it really shows. The flavors are better, the food is juicier, and there is less chance of burning the food.

The following table will help you to follow the recipes accurately and keep the grill at the appropriate temperature, when using both gas and charcoal grills:

High heat: . . . . .550°F or higher
Medium-high heat: . . . . .450 to 550°F
Medium: . . . . .350 to 450°F
Medium-low: . . . . .250 to 350°F
Low: . . . . .less than 250°F

CAUTIONARY NOTES

SAFETY TIPS FOR PLANKING

It is important to use caution when planking. Even properly soaked planks can catch fire. Planking is a lot of fun, but please exercise caution and common sense when preparing these recipes. Follow the rules and you shouldn't have any trouble.

Always remember; planks are made of wood, have a tendency to smoke and possibly catch fire. Smoke is good; fire is bad.

RECOMMENDED SAFETY EQUIPMENT

- High-heat thermometer suitable for the grill.
- Squeeze or spray bottle filled with water.
- Garden hose.
- Fire extinguisher, just in case.
- Phone: to dial 911, better safe than sorry.
- Goggles: swimming goggles, snow goggles, or sunglasses will work but some type of eye protection is necessary when checking planks during smoking and when removing from the grill.
- Sturdy pair of long, well-made grilling tongs. Tongs need to be able to hold the weight of a plank with food on it.
- Large, metal container filled with water, should a fire break out.
- Thick, heat-resistant barbecue gloves to keep your hands safe.

SAFETY TIPS

- All planks should be made of natural, pure, untreated wood.
- Soak all planks in cold water for a minimum of 1 hour prior to planking.
- Never brush planks with any type of oil; this is literally adding fuel to a piece of wood that can potentially ignite.
- Keep all children and pets away from grill while planking.
- Never leave your grill unattended once planking has commenced. Keep to your post and be prepared.
- Soak used planks in water for a minimum of 30 minutes before putting in the garbage.
- Consider wind direction when plank grilling and adjust position of grill as needed.
- Should a plank ignite, reduce temperature or turn burners off. Lift the lid and douse flames with the spray bottle that is ALWAYS standing by. Replace lid, and resume plank grilling.
- Transfer hot planks from the grill to a heat-proof platter, another raw, soaked plank, or baking sheet to prevent burning tabletops or counters, as the underside of the plank is very hot.
- Always transfer cooked food onto a new, soaked plank or serving platter outside before bringing food inside. I like to use funky-shaped planks that we have cut specially for doing the final service.
- Be careful!

PLANKING TIPS

- Always soak planks in cold water for a minimum of 1 hour or up to 24 hours before planking.
- Soak planks in different liquids to impart different flavors. Try wine, beer, or juice. Herbs and spices will also add a new dimension to the flavor of the wood.
- Remove bark from planks as the bark produces a bitter smoke.
- Use sandpaper to remove any splinters from the wood before rinsing and soaking the plank.
- Quick and easy recipes are best for charcoal barbecues. Having to add more charcoal to the grill means losing precious smoke and increasing the cook time.
- Neither the plank nor the food needs to be flipped or rotated once on the grill.
- Refrain from opening the grill lid too often when planking. This will keep the beautiful smoke in and the cooking time on schedule.
- When mashed potatoes/vegetables are too fresh, they will run off the plank leaving a nasty mess on the grill, so prepare them the day before planking.
- Try cutting planks into different shapes for an impressive presentation.
- Never waste leftovers! Get creative or make a sandwich. Leftover planked salmon makes an out-of-this-world salmon salad sandwich with the addition of a little mayonnaise.
- Planking takes time, so be patient, it will all be worth it in the end!

VARIETALS OF WOOD

Suitable woods for plank grilling are much like fine wines; there are many different types and they vary from region to region. The Pacific Northwest produces a great deal of western red cedar and alder; maple and oak are abundant in Canada and the northern U.S.; hickory and nut woods are common in the southern U.S.; and fruit woods (including apple, peach, and pear) are available in many parts of Canada and the U.S.

Western red cedar is the most commonly used wood to make planks. It imparts a sweet smoke, is especially aromatic, and is the most versatile for plank grilling.

Semi-hard or hardwood (e.g., western red cedar, maple, and oak) are the most suitable for planks, as they have less sap and do not burn as quickly as softwoods. Avoid using softwoods, such as pine, as they tend to produce a bitter smoke, resulting in Pine Sol–tasting food. Bark also imparts a bitter flavor, so be sure to remove all bark before soaking planks. Bark also tends to ignite more easily than clean wood.

Here is a list of the different woods I recommend using for plank grilling, as well as the flavors they impart, suggested flavorings for soaking, and suggested foods for each variety of plank:

HICKORY—a hardwood with a very bold flavor from the southern U.S. It's very much a "good ole boys" kind of wood. Hickory can be difficult to find, so when you do find it buy a ton and hold onto it. It works really well when slowly plank grilling a large cut of meat over low heat. For soaking, use water, beer, bourbon, ginger ale, Coca Cola, apple juice, pineapple juice, or cabernet sauvignon. These planks are best used with pork (ribs, chops, and bacon), turkey, ham, steaks, game (venison, ostrich, buffalo, pheasant), and portobello mushrooms.

MAPLE—a hardwood with a subtle, sweet smoke and a nice balance. Soak this plank in water, apple juice, chardonnay, cabernet sauvignon, honey brown lager, or even a maple-flavored lager. Use maple for plank grilling poultry (chicken, turkey, duck, quail), trout, salmon, arctic char, pizza, and steaks.

PECAN—a hardwood with mildly sweet and nutty flavors from the south. These planks are especially hard to find, but well worth the search. Try soaking this plank in water, strong dark beer like Guinness, cabernet sauvignon or merlot, chardonnay, apple juice, or ginger ale. Pecan is awesome for plank baking desserts, fruits, vegetables, mushrooms, quail, chicken, turkey, and pork.

RED OAK—a hardwood with a deeply rustic smoke flavor; it's best paired with strong flavors. Cover this plank with water, cabernet sauvignon, merlot, India pale ale, grape juice, cranberry juice, or orange juice. Grill beef, game, poultry, cheese, and desserts on this plank.

WESTERN RED CEDAR—a semi-hard, aromatic and sweet wood from the Pacific Northwest. It is easy to find and perfect for plank grilling. Cedar produces big smoke and big flavor. Try soaking the plank in water, chardonnay, hard cider, Pilsner, Dr. Pepper or cherry juice. This plank complements salmon, seafood, cheese, poultry, game meats, beef, pork, veal, and lamb. Cedar is even great for fruits, vegetables, and desserts. Like I said before, cedar is a very versatile plank.

ALDER—a semi-hardwood with a delicate and slightly sweet smoke flavor from the Pacific Northwest. Alder is best when soaked in water, chardonnay, sauvignon blanc, Riesling, pinot noir, apple juice, lager or ale. Alder is great for cooking vegetables, salmon, halibut, arctic char, pork, chicken, and fruit.

APPLE—a semi-hardwood that produces a subtle fruity and sweet smoke. For soaking, use water, apple juice, apple ale, apple wine, apple cider, chardonnay, pinot noir, or pineapple juice. Use apple planks for planking poultry, fish, shellfish, pork chops and pork tenderloin, veal, assorted vegetables, and fruit.

CHERRY—a semi-hardwood that creates a tart, fruity smoke. Try soaking cherry wood in water, pinot noir, Shiraz, sauvignon blanc, chardonnay, cherry whiskey, Cherry Coke, or cherry juice. Cherry planks are perfect for venison, beef, turkey, pork chops, pork tenderloin, cheese, and fruit.

MESQUITE—a hardwood that lets out a sweet smoke. It is an exotic wood, making it hard to find but is great for long cooking time due to its thickness. It is extra delicious when soaked in water, cider, pineapple juice, lemonade, beer or ginger ale. Mesquite is a strong flavor so it works best with beef, pork, and poultry.

WHERE TO FIND AND BUY PLANKS

I've been planking for nearly 20 years now and when I started doing this there weren't many places you could buy planks. In fact, there was only one place I could get planks—the lumberyard. I would go in and buy a great big piece of wood and ask the guys to cut it into 10-inch long planks. This obviously piqued their curiosity and they would ask how I was going to use them. When I explained I was cooking on the wood, it really opened a floodgate of questions. They began to think I was crazy until other customers, seemingly normal people, were also asking for their wood to be cut into planks. All these years later, the lumberyard is still the best place to get planks.

There are a few more options out there these days. Many grocery stores and gourmet shops carry planks, as well as many home improvement–type stores. However, they usually only have untreated western red cedar. While cedar is a great wood to plank with, there are so many other wonderful flavors of wood. Red oak and maple are hardwoods that produce a good amount of smoke for long periods of time and don't usually ignite. Alder has a slightly nutty flavor and hickory is a great hardwood with a not-too-sweet flavor. These varieties of wood are harder to find, but worth the search as they each impart a different flavor to food.

Planks are available in different sizes and thickness. Use small planks for small portions, wider planks for roasts, and longer planks for longer items like whole sides of salmon. The length and width of a plank is not as important as the thickness of a plank.

Thickness is the most important thing to consider when buying planks. The thinner the plank, the less amount of time it can stay on the grill. Recipes that have a quick cooking time can get by with a thin plank, but a longer cooking time will either need a regular or thick plank. Every recipe in this book will specify what thickness of plank to use.

THIN PLANK
Approximately ¼ to ½ in. thick
Maximum of 15 to 20 minutes of cooking time
(mashed potatoes, risotto, vegetables, garlic)

REGULAR PLANK
Approximately ¾ in. thick
20 to 60 minutes of cooking time
(salmon or other fish fillets, steaks, pork loin, ribs, tuna, roast chicken and game)

THICK PLANK
Approximately 1 in. or more thick
60 minutes plus of cooking time
(turkey, prime rib, veal roast, pork loin roast, whole fish)

NOTE: Thin planks tend to warp when heated. To avoid warping, place the plank over high heat (without food) for a couple of minutes, turn the plank over and place the food on the lightly heated side. Hardwoods are less likely to warp than semi-hard woods, but take this easy precaution just to be safe. Soaking the plank for a longer amount of time will also help to prevent the plank from warping. Why is warping such a big deal? Well, when a plank warps, the food will most likely roll off onto the grill, make a huge mess and screw up your dinner.

Note: It is very important that you NEVER cook with treated wood. Not even if you have a heap of scrap wood left over from a building project or find railway ties on the side of the tracks. Use only untreated, 100 per cent pure, natural wood. I'm sure this all seems like common sense, but you would be surprised at the number of people whom I have seen using leftover wood from the cedar deck they just had built to plank grill their food. A while back I was at a party where the host could have been a bit more gracious. He was very boisterous about how good his plank salmon was and that I didn't know as much on the topic as everyone thought I did. It was then that I kindly put him in his place by telling him that the reason his fish smelt like a freshly painted washroom was because of the treated cedar deck scraps he had cooked it on. A couple of weeks later he attended one of my grilling and barbecue classes.

Another great place to find planks is on the Internet. Google "grilling planks," and you will find an outrageous number of planks, planking recipes, and even me, Ted Reader, at www.tedreader.com. Some of the major distributors of cedar and other wood variety planks are major grocery stores, specialty food shops, and specialty barbecue supply stores. Home and garden stores (Home Depot, Lowe's, Canadian Tire, Home Hardware, Bass Pro Shops, Ace Hardware, Gander Mountain, Pro Hardware and Rona, just to name a few) also have a good selection of planks. Don't forget your local lumberyard as they will have the hard-to-come-by woods and can cut them in a variety of lengths.

The following is a list of some of the folks that I have come in contact with over the years regarding processing and selling planks:

TED READER'S WORLD FAMOUS BBQ

80 Sherbourne Street, Suite 106
Toronto, Ontario
Canada M5A 2R1
Tel: 416-635-9889
Fax: 416-635-7766
E-mail: les@eventrix.ca
www.tedreader.com

Montana Cross Cut Planks

www.montanagrills.com

Exotic Woods Inc.

2483 Industrial Road
Burlington, Ontario
Tel: 905-335-8066
Fax: 905-335-7080
info@exotic-woods.com
www.exotic-woods.com

Fire & Flavor Grilling Co.

Gina Knox the Queen of Planks
328 Commerce Blvd., Suite 8
Bogart, Georgia, USA 30622
www.fireandflavor.com
I love your planks.

Currier & Reeves, LLC

The Red Oak Plank Dudes
P.O. Box 116
Thayer, Missouri, USA 65791
Toll Free: (888) 886-7455
Tel: (417) 264-3587
Fax: (417) 264-2723
E-mail: info@grillplanks.com
www.grillplanks.com

Smokinlicious

110 North 2nd Street
Olean, New York 14760
Tel: 1-800-941-5054
Fax Number: 1-716-372-0439
E-mail: Info@SmokinLicious.com
www.smokinlicious.com

Northwest Plank Co.

All Northwest
383 Mill Creek Road
Longview, WA 98632
Tel: 360-423-6216
Fax: 360-577-6379
www.nwplank.com

Great Lakes Grilling Co.

2680 Walker Ave., Suite C
Grand Rapids, MI 49544
Toll Free: 877-791-8600
Fax: 616-791-6501
info@greatlakesgrilling.com
www.greatlakesgrilling.com

North American Cedar

Spokane Valley, WA
Tel: (877) 262-6937
Fax: (509) 893-8632
E-mail: info@northamericancedar.com
www.nacedar.com

Nature's Gourmet™

Mission Viejo, CA
Toll Free: 866-522-3093
Fax: 949-855-0860
E-mail: info@naturesgourmet.com
www.naturesgourmet.com

Main Grilling Woods

c/o Lexington Outdoor Inc.
33 Lakeview Street
Lincoln, Maine 04457
Tel: 207-794-8232
E-mail: sales@lexingtonoutdoors.com
www.mainegrillingwoods.com

Montana Bounty Foods

P.O. Box 8510
Kalispell, MT 59904
Toll Free: (866) 722-2469
Fax: (406) 756-2602
www.bountyfoods.com

Enyeart Cedar Products

Tel: 800-551-6657
Fax: 503-697-9385
E-mail: info@enyeartcedar.com

SOAKING PLANKS

It is extremely important that planks are soaked in cold water before grilling, for both safety and flavor reasons. A minimum of 1 hour in a cold bath is necessary, 2 hours is preferred and 4 hours is ideal. Place the plank in a large bin, cover with a cold liquid and top with something heavy to keep the plank submerged. Soaking will keep the plank from igniting and it produces a clean and flavorful smoke.

FLAVORING PLANKS

Try adding extra flavor to planks by soaking them in different liquids. A 1:1 ratio works best; 1 part water to 1 part flavoring liquid. Soak planks for 2 to 4 hours to really get the flavors soaked in there. Try apple cider for apple wood planks, red and white wine are always a success, even fruit juice like pineapple or cranberry work well. Beer is awesome when paired with ribs and bourbon is just the thing for burgers.

Salt is added to food for many reasons, but the most important is that salt brings out the natural flavors of food; it's no different when added to wood. Season the planks with coarse sea salt prior to placing food on the plank.

Have fun, play around; try adding fresh herbs or grape leaves between the plank and the food. Cinnamon sticks, whole nutmeg, or vanilla beans will also add another dimension of flavor to your food.

Beer

Red wine

Water

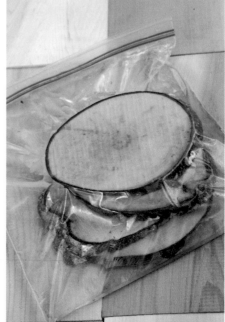

THE PLANK ROASTING PAN

Once you've mastered the art of making a plank roasting pan, you may want to get a little creative. Try making a shepherd's pie, brownies, or even tuna casserole in your plank roasting pan. Have fun and make it delicious!

1	plank, 12-inch (30 cm) x 8-inch (20 cm), minimum ¾-inch (2 cm) thick
4	uniform cedar shims, minimum 12-inch (30 cm) to 14-inch (35 cm) long and 4-inch (10 cm) wide
8 to 16	1-inch (2.5 cm) flat-head nails (no fancy finishing nails)

On a flat work surface place the plank on one of its long edges. Lay one shim on the edge of the plank, ensuring the thick end of the shim is square with the corner and the edge; this will be the bottom of the roasting pan. Hammer a nail about 1 inch (2.5 cm). from the corner of the plank as close to the center of the width as possible. Repeat at the other end of the shim with a second nail. You may choose to hammer a nail into the center as well. Trim any excess shim hanging off the edge and discard. Repeat with the remaining three edges of the plank to make a 3–4-inch (8–10 cm) deep roasting pan.

When baking or adding very fluid ingredients into this pan, it's a good idea to add a few more nails around the corners of the shims, just for insurance. This can be a little tricky since the shims are thin and split easily when the nail doesn't go in just right. Stick it out, the first time is tricky but it's amazing how simple this is to make the second time around.

THE COFFIN (OR SMOKING BOX)

This plank is used for planked turkey, which means you need to have a large barbecue with a high lid. Oak and maple are the perfect hardwoods for this concept but western red cedar works well, too. Cooking a whole turkey takes a while and you'll need a wood that will stand up to the extended cooking time. Remember to use only untreated wood. A vice or an extra pair of hands will come in handy for the assembly of this box.

6	planks, 12-inch (30 cm) x 8-inch (20 cm) x 1-inch (2.5 cm) thick (2 sides, top and bottom)
2	planks, 16-inch (40 cm) x 7-inch (18 cm) x 1-inch (2.5 cm) thick (2 sides)
16 to 24	2-inch (5 cm) flat-head nails (no fancy finishing nails)

Soak planks in cold water for a minimum of 1 hour. (Note: soaking planks prior to building your plank coffin is much easier than soaking a huge, assembled box.)

The dimensions of the finished box, with the lid, are 18-inch (45 cm) x 12-inch (30 cm) x 10-inch (25 cm). Check that this will fit inside your closed grill and that your bird of choice will fit in the box.

Start with four 12-inch (30 cm) x 8-inch (20 cm) planks. Lay 2 planks flat on a work surface, shorter ends of the 12-inch (30 cm) plank together, creating a 12-inch (30 cm) x 16-inch (40 cm) base. This will be the bottom of the box. Nail a 12-inch (30 cm) x 8-inch (20 cm) plank, using 2 or 3 nails, to the outside edge of each of the planks also working with the 12-inch (30 cm) sides. This will give you 2 "L" shapes facing each other. Slot the 16-inch (40 cm) x 7-inch (18 cm) planks onto the bottom of the box, between the 2 sides to create the final 2 sides. They should fit snugly. Nail into place. Flip over the box and secure the bottom of the box to the sides with more nails. Once you have your turkey in place, use the two remaining 12-inch (30 cm) x 8-inch (20 cm) planks as a lid.

HOLY PLANK

A Forstner drill bit is the best for this kind of thing. Unlike a spade bit, a Forstner will make a clean well in the wood with no hole in the middle.

1   thick, regular plank, 12-inch (30 cm) x 8-inch (20 cm), minimum 1-inch (5 cm) thick

Secure the plank to a work surface. Place the drill bit to the edge of the plank to gauge how far you can drill into the plank without going all the way through. Remember it.

Drill 32 holes (4 rows of 8 holes) using a ¾-inch (2 cm) or 1-inch (2.5 cm) Forstner drill bit. The holes don't have to be lined up perfectly—it's barbecue; relax!

Rinse the plank thoroughly to remove all sawdust before soaking in water.

Once the plank is thoroughly soaked, fill the reservoirs with water, beer, cider, juice, wine, or even soda. The liquid keeps the food moist while planking because it creates a smoke-flavored steam as the liquid in the holes evaporates. Be sure to keep the reservoirs full for the duration of cooking. This is the best plank for slow roasting; the results are moist and succulent every time!

THE VERTICAL PLANK

I have always found that when grilling kebabs, satay, spedinis or any skewered meat, the wooden skewers tend to burn up on the grill. The only solution is to use metal skewers, but they are such a pain in the butt to clean!

I got to thinking: why not create a plank that allows the skewers to stand *vertically* on the grill? The plank will add great smoke flavor to your skewered food and it prevent the skewers from catching fire.

The next thing ya know, good old Ted's got a drill in one hand and plank in the other and the vertical plank was born!

1   regular plank, 12-inch (30 cm) x 8-inch (20 cm), minimum ¾-inch (2 cm) thick

Secure the plank to a work surface with a clamp or vice. Put a second plank underneath just in case you drill too far and go past the vertical plank. This way you don't drill holes in your picnic table or something you know you're not supposed to drill on. Do you know what I am talking about guys?

Drill straight down onto secured plank approximately three-quarters of the way through the wood. Make 18 evenly spaced holes (6 rows along the length and 3 across, with 1–2 inches (2.5–5 cm) between each hole). When all holes are drilled, brush off any excess sawdust. You now have a vertical plank!

NOTES ON THE VERTICAL PLANK:

- Compare the size of the skewer being used to drill bits before drilling any holes. Use the bit that is closest to the size of the skewer; go bigger rather than smaller, but not too much bigger.
- For the plank listed above, 18 skewers fit perfectly. You could squeeze 24 onto the plank, but the smoke flavor is better when there's room between the skewers for the smoke to circulate.
- Soak wooden skewers in water prior to skewering food.
- When skewering meats, leave 1–2 inches (2.5–5 cm) open space at the pointed end of each skewer so that it will fit in the plank's support holes.
- Use skewers that are 8–10 inches (20–25 cm) long and leave enough space on the blunt end of the skewer so that you can easily grab the cooked skewers directly off the plank. It's a great presentation for serving your guests!
- Make sure the skewers, when inserted into the vertical plank, will allow enough clearance so that the grill lid will close without pushing on the skewers.

PLANK WITH LEGS FOR FISH AROUND THE CAMPFIRE

There are a variety of ways to build this type of stand. I made mine using a longer, thinner plank for the legs.

2	1-inch (2.5 cm) nails
2	plank pieces, 14-inch (35 cm) x 1½-inch (4 cm) x ¼-inch (5 mm) (the legs)
1	plank, 12-inch (30 cm) x 8-inch (20 cm) x 1-inch (2.5 cm)

Use one nail to secure each leg to either side of the shorter plank, near the top corner. Nail into the 1-inch (2.5 cm) thick side. These legs are adjustable to allow for angle adjustments of the plank around an open fire—essentially the temperature control.

Nail the food to the board and position about 1–2 feet (30–60 cm) from the hot coals. Adjust the angle and position as necessary.

CHILI PEPPER GRILL PLANK

The chili pepper grill was designed to hold stuffed jalapeno peppers over the grill. It allows the peppers to roast without burning and to prevent the stuffing mixture (which is usually loaded with cheese) from oozing out all over the grill.

The original chili grill, which is made of metal, doesn't add any flavor to the food, so I have created a plank chili grill so that when you grill stuffed jalapenos, they'll have a wonderful smoke flavor from the wood.

2	½-inch (1 cm) thick, 6-inch (15 cm) square cedar, maple, oak, hickory, or mesquite planks	2
6	small nails	6
1	12-inch (30 cm) x 6-inch (15 cm) x ½-inch (1 cm) cedar, maple, oak, hickory or mesquite planks	1

Prepare the large plank as you would prepare the Holy Plank (p. 39) but instead of creating reservoirs to hold liquid, drill the holes all the way through.

Nail the 6-inch (15 cm) boards to the narrow ends of the plank to create support legs, using 3 nails per side. Attach these legs halfway up the plank. This allows the peppers room to poke through the other side (see photo). Soak plank in water prior to use.

APPETIZERS

SEAFOOD PLANK SEASONING

½ cup	light brown sugar	125 mL
¼ cup	coarsely ground fresh black pepper	60 mL
¼ cup	kosher salt or coarsely ground sea salt	60 mL
3 Tbsp	granulated onion	45 mL
2 Tbsp	mustard seeds, cracked	30 mL
1 Tbsp	dried dill weed	15 mL
1 Tbsp	dill seed	15 mL
1 Tbsp	coriander seed	15 mL
1 Tbsp	lemon pepper seasoning	15 mL
2 tsp	granulated garlic	10 mL

This seasoning spice blend is all you need when plank grilling, whether it be salmon, cheese, steak, tuna, breakfast, dessert, or a burger. It features a blend of sugar and spice that really makes everything nice.

• In a large bowl, mix all ingredients together. Transfer to a tightly sealed container and store in a cool, dry place for up to 6 months.

MAKES APPROXIMATELY 1½ CUPS (375 ML)

BONE DUST BBQ SEASONING

½ cup	paprika	125 mL
¼ cup	chili powder	60 mL
3 Tbsp	salt	45 mL
2 Tbsp	ground coriander	30 mL
2 Tbsp	garlic powder	30 mL
2 Tbsp	granulated white sugar	30 mL
2 Tbsp	mild Indian curry powder	30 mL
2 Tbsp	dry hot mustard powder (Keen's or Coleman's)	30 mL
1 Tbsp	freshly ground black pepper	15 mL
1 Tbsp	dried basil	15 mL
1 Tbsp	dried thyme	15 mL
1 Tbsp	ground cumin	15 mL
1 Tbsp	cayenne	15 mL

Bone Dust BBQ Seasoning is used in many of the recipes in this book, so make a big batch and use it all summer long.

• In a large bowl, mix all ingredients together. Transfer to a tightly sealed container and store in a cool, dry place for up to 6 months.

MAKES APPROXIMATELY 2¼ CUPS (560 ML)

SWEET SPICE RUB

1 cup	brown sugar	250 mL
¼ cup	coarse kosher salt	60 mL
3 Tbsp	coarsely ground black pepper	45 mL
2 Tbsp	coarsely ground white pepper	30 mL
2 Tbsp	mustard seeds	30 mL
2 Tbsp	cracked coriander seeds	30 mL
2 Tbsp	garlic powder	30 mL
2 Tbsp	onion powder	30 mL
2 Tbsp	pink peppercorns, cracked	30 mL
1 Tbsp	crushed red chili flakes	15 mL
1 Tbsp	dill seed	15 mL

• In a large bowl, mix all ingredients together. Transfer to a tightly sealed container and store in a cool, dry place for up to 6 months.

MAKES APPROXIMATELY 2½ CUPS (625 ML)

CEDAR PLANK–ROASTED GARLIC SOUP
WITH PLANK-ROASTED BEER BRATS

2	regular cedar, maple, oak or hickory planks, soaked in water	2
6	heads garlic	6
4–6	bratwurst sausages, 5 oz (150 g) each	4–6
2 Tbsp	butter	30 mL
1	medium parsnip, peeled and diced	1
4	large potatoes, peeled and diced	4
2	leeks, white part only, well washed and diced	2
1 cup	Sleeman Honey Brown Lager	250 mL
4 cups	chicken stock	1 L
1 Tbsp	fresh chopped thyme	15 mL
¼ cup	fresh chopped Italian parsley	60 mL
1 cup	grated Emmenthal cheese	250 mL

• Preheat grill to medium heat. Place the garlic heads on a flat surface. With a sharp knife cut the tops off to expose the tips of the garlic cloves. Place the garlic heads, cut side down, onto a plank. Place on the grill and close the lid. Roast for about 1 hour until the garlic cloves are golden brown and very soft. Remove from grill and cool. Separate the roasted cloves from the skins and discard the skins; set cloves aside.

• Place the brats onto the plank, place on the grill and close the lid. Roast *slow and low* for about 30 to 40 minutes, until fully cooked and golden brown.

• Remove from heat and allow to cool completely. Slice thinly; set aside.

• In a large saucepan, melt the butter over medium heat. Add the diced parsnip, potatoes and leeks. Cook for 5 to 6 minutes to soften, stirring well. Add the roasted garlic and the beer. Cook for 3 to 4 minutes, stirring well. Add the chicken stock and bring to a boil. Reduce heat and simmer for 30 minutes, until the potatoes are fully cooked and tender. Remove from heat and purée; stir in the thyme and parsley.

• Serve immediately garnished with Emmenthal cheese and plank-smoked bratwurst sausage slices. Serve with ice-cold Sleeman Honey Brown Lager.

SERVES 8

PLANK-SMOKED HALIBUT AND LOBSTER CHOWDER WITH DILL PESTO

1	regular plank, soaked in water	1
DILL PESTO:		
1	bunch dill, washed, large stems removed	1
¼ cup	olive oil	60 mL
2 Tbsp	lemon juice	30 mL
¼ cup	grated Parmesan cheese	60 mL
2	cloves garlic	2
¼ cup	pine nuts	60 mL
1 lb	lobster meat, drained and squeezed of any excess moisture	500 g
4	small shallots, finely diced	4
2 Tbsp	Seafood Plank Seasoning (p. 45)	30 mL
1 Tbsp	lemon juice	15 mL
1 tsp	lemon zest	5 mL
1 lb	fresh halibut	500 g
¼ cup	butter	60 mL
1 cup	diced, smoked ham	250 mL
3	cloves garlic, minced	3
1	yellow onion, finely diced	1
2	stalks celery, finely diced	2
1	large leek, white only, well-washed and finely diced	1
4	Yukon Gold potatoes, peeled and diced into ½-inch (1 cm) cubes	4
3 Tbsp	all-purpose flour	45 mL
3 cups	chicken stock	750 mL
2 cups	whipping cream	500 mL
	Salt and freshly ground black pepper	
	Crusty bread	

Nothing beats a big bowl of chowder, especially when the chowder is loaded with lightly plank-smoked seafood.

DILL PESTO: In a food processor or blender, combine the dill, olive oil, lemon juice, Parmesan cheese, garlic and pine nuts. Purée until smooth; set aside.

• Preheat grill to medium-high heat. Mix together the lobster, shallots, Seafood Plank Seasoning, lemon juice and lemon zest. Place the halibut onto the plank and spread lobster mixture evenly over the halibut.

• Place the plank onto the grill and close the lid. Plank bake for 20 minutes, until the fish flakes easily with a fork. Remove from grill and allow to cool to room temperature; set aside.

• Melt the butter in a large saucepan set over medium-high heat. Add the ham, garlic, onion, celery, leek and potatoes. Sauté ham and vegetables for 4 to 5 minutes, until tender. Add the flour and stir with a wooden spoon until well combined.

• Add the chicken stock a little at a time, stirring well after each addition until mixture is smooth. Bring to a boil; reduce heat to medium-low and simmer for 30 minutes, stirring occasionally, until the potatoes are tender.

• Stir in cream and return to a slow boil. Cut the cooled, planked halibut into ½-inch (1 cm) chunks. Gently stir the fish into the chowder. Season to taste with salt and pepper. Garnish with reserved dill mixture and serve immediately with crusty bread.

SERVES 8

TIP: This recipe is made with lobster-topped halibut but feel free to use leftover planked salmon, sea bass, shrimp, scallops, cod and/or haddock.

CRAB-STUFFED SUPER JUMBO SHRIMP

1	12-inch (30 cm) maple plank, soaked in water	1
½ cup	crabmeat	125 mL
½ cup	softened cream cheese	125 mL
¼ cup	finely chopped crisp, cooked double-smoked bacon	60 mL
¼ cup	fresh bread crumbs	60 mL
2	small shallots, minced	2
2 Tbsp	chopped fresh herbs, such as dill and/or chives	30 mL
1 Tbsp	lemon juice	15 mL
1 tsp + 2 tsp	Bone Dust BBQ Seasoning (p. 46)	15 mL
4	jumbo shrimp, peeled and deveined, tail-on, 3/5 count	4

• Blend the crabmeat, cream cheese, bacon, bread crumbs, shallots, herbs, lemon juice and 1 tsp Bone Dust BBQ Seasoning; set aside. Preheat grill to medium-high heat.

• Rinse shrimp under cold water and pat dry. Place shrimp onto a cutting board. Using the incision from deveining the shrimp as a guide, butterfly the shrimp from the top leaving about ½-inch (1 cm) intact at the thickest end, forming a large pocket in the shrimp. Season with BBQ Bone Dust Seasoning.

• Lightly pack about ⅓ cup (75 mL) of the crab mixture into the cavity of each shrimp.

• Place stuffed shrimp onto prepared plank. Place plank on grill and close lid. When plank starts to crackle, turn heat down to medium-low. It will take about 20 to 25 minutes to cook the shrimp and stuffing. Remove plank from grill and serve immediately.

SERVES 4

CRESCENT CITY OYSTERS ROCKEFELLER

2	regular cedar, maple or alder planks, soaked in water	2
24	fresh large oysters (Malpeque from PEI or Gulf Oysters from Louisiana are ideal)	24
1	large, sweet onion, cut into 6 wedges	1
2 Tbsp	olive oil	30 mL
1 Tbsp	Bone Dust BBQ Seasoning (p. 46)	15 mL
2 Tbsp	butter	30 mL
8 cups	baby spinach	2 L
½ tsp	cracked black pepper	2 mL
4 oz	Sleeman India Pale Ale	60 mL
2 Tbsp	softened butter	30 mL
1 cup	crawfish meat, thawed and coarsely chopped	250 mL
½ cup + 2 Tbsp	grated Parmesan cheese	125 mL + 30 mL
1 cup	grated Emmenthal cheese	250 mL

This recipe works best with large, fresh oysters since the bigger the oyster is when fresh, the more plump and juicy it will be after planking. That said, when choosing large oysters, don't compromise on quality.

• Shuck the oysters and rinse the shells under hot water to remove any sand; remove any bits of oyster meat remaining on the shell. Reserve the shells and meat separately; can be held in the refrigerator for up to 2 days.

• Preheat grill to medium-high. Toss the onion in the olive oil and BBQ seasoning.

• Grill for 6 to 8 minutes per side or until lightly charred and tender. Remove from grill and cool before coarsely chopping; set aside.

• In a large frying pan, melt the butter over medium-high heat. Add the spinach, cracked black pepper and beer. Cook for 1 to 2 minutes, until the spinach is wilted. Remove from heat. Drain off any excess moisture and allow mixture to cool to room temperature. Squeeze spinach mixture to remove any excess moisture.

• Chop the spinach. Transfer to a bowl and fold in chopped onion, soft butter, crawfish meat and ½ cup (125 mL) Parmesan cheese; set aside.

• Place 12 pretty oyster shells, inside up, on a flat surface. Place a fresh oyster in each shell. Spoon 2 Tbsp (30 mL) of spinach mixture over top of each one and top with another oyster. Mix remaining Parmesan cheese with shredded Emmenthal cheese. Sprinkle evenly over top of the oysters.

• Arrange the filled oyster shells onto 1 or 2 plank(s); position the remaining shells, outside up, around the filled oysters on the planks, to provide balance.

• Preheat grill to high heat. Place the plank(s) on the grill and close the lid. Plank bake for 15 to 20 minutes, until the oysters are heated through and the cheese is golden brown. Remove from grill and serve.

Serve with Sleeman India Pale Ale.

SERVES 4

GRILL-ROASTED PINE NEEDLE MUSSELS

Mess of pine needles (like a bucketful), soaked in water for 15 minutes

5 lb	fresh mussels, cleaned and debearded	2.5 kg
3 Tbsp	sea salt	45 mL
1	bunch fresh rosemary, leaves removed from stalks	1
1	bottle (350 mL) Sleeman Honey Brown Lager	1
	Black pepper	
	Drawn butter*	

This recipe can get a bit messy, so to make cleanup fast and easy, place a foil baking sheet under the grate before preheating the grill. It will catch the pine needles and ash and prevent the gas valves from becoming clogged.

• Preheat grill to high heat. Season mussels with sea salt. Mix together 3 to 4 handfuls of pine needles with the rosemary.

• Place the mussels on the grill. Cover with the pine needle/rosemary mixture and close the lid. This will allow the mussels to begin to roast and smoke and keep the pine needles from catching fire. Let the mussels roast for 8 to 10 minutes. **NOTE:** Do this in a well-vented area.

• Carefully open grill lid and stand back. The pine needles will ignite and burn up.

• When the flames have died down, use a bellows or piece of newsprint and fan as much of the ash as you can from the mussels. Drizzle evenly with beer.

• Transfer mussels to a serving platter. Discard unopened mussels. Season open mussels with pepper. Serve with drawn butter and extra-chilled beer.

*TIP: Drawn butter is also known as clarified butter. To make drawn butter, place butter in a saucepan and melt very slowly over low heat. This will cause the water in the butter to evaporate and the milk solids to sink to the bottom. Skim any foam off the top and discard. Pour the golden liquid into a separate bowl, being careful to leave the milk solids behind; discard solids.

SERVES 4 TO 6

SMOKED SALMON–WRAPPED SCALLOPS
WITH PISTACHIO HORSERADISH CRUST

1	regular maple plank, soaked in water	1
½ cup	ground pistachio nuts	125 mL
3	cloves garlic, minced	3
2	green onions, finely chopped	2
½ cup	diced cucumber	125 mL
2 Tbsp	prepared horseradish	30 mL
2 Tbsp	honey	30 mL
2 Tbsp	lemon juice	30 mL
2 Tbsp	olive oil	30 mL
	Sea salt and freshly ground black pepper	
12	fresh jumbo scallops	12
12	slices Vodka Maple Salmon Gravlax or store-bought smoked salmon	12

The scallops in this recipe should be uniform in size and as big as possible.

• In a bowl, mix together the pistachio nuts, garlic, green onions, cucumber, horseradish, honey, lemon juice and olive oil. Season with salt and pepper to taste.

• Using a paper towel, pat the scallops dry and then season with salt and pepper. Wrap a slice of gravlax or smoked salmon around each scallop and secure with a toothpick. Crust the topside of the scallop generously with the pistachio mixture.

• Preheat the grill to high heat. Place plank on grill and close lid. Heat the wood for 3 to 5 minutes, until it crackles and smokes. Open the grill and place the scallops, crust side up, on the plank, spaced about ½-inch (1 cm) apart. Close the lid and bake for 6 to 8 minutes, until the scallops are golden brown and the crust crispy.

• Serve with chilled shots of Finlandia Vodka

SERVES 4 MAINS OR 12 APPETIZERS

VODKA MAPLE SALMON GRAVLAX

½ cup	Finlandia Vodka	125 mL
¼ cup	maple syrup	60 mL
1	boneless, skin on, scaled Atlantic salmon fillet, 1½–2 lb (750 g–1 kg)	1
3	green onions, finely chopped	3
1	bunch fresh cilantro, finely chopped	1
¾ cup	kosher salt	175 mL
½ cup	granulated sugar	125 mL
2 Tbsp	freshly cracked black pepper	30 mL
2 Tbsp	Seafood Plank Seasoning (p. 45)	30 mL

• In a bowl, combine vodka and maple syrup. Lay the side of salmon, skin side down, in a 2-inch (5 cm) deep pan and pour over the vodka mixture.

• In a bowl, combine the green onions, cilantro, salt, sugar, pepper and Seafood Plank Seasoning. Sprinkle this mixture evenly over the salmon, pressing seasoning in lightly and making sure flesh is covered completely. Cover pan with enough plastic wrap to overlap the edges of the pan by several inches. Place another pan over top of the salmon, weight it with a couple of planks and refrigerate for 24 hours.

• Remove salmon from fridge and unwrap. Scrape away and discard salt mixture. Rinse salmon very briefly under cold water and pat dry with paper towel. Slice thinly, starting at the tail end. Cover any unused portion tightly with plastic wrap and refrigerate. Gravlax will keep for one week in the refrigerator or for 3 months frozen.

SERVES 8 TO 12

PINEAPPLE PLANK SHRIMP CAKES

1	Cajun-style injector syringe*	1
2 lb	raw shrimp, peeled and deveined, 21/25 per pound	1 kg
2	green onions, finely diced	2
1	red onion, finely diced	1
1	red pepper, finely diced	1
½ cup	Southern Comfort liquer	125 mL
2 Tbsp	cilantro	30 mL
1 Tbsp	Sambal olek chili sauce	15 mL
1 Tbsp	rice vinegar	15 mL
1 Tbsp	lime juice	15 mL
1 Tbsp	olive oil	15 mL
2 tsp	minced ginger	10 mL
1 tsp	fish sauce	5 mL
1	ripe but firm pineapple	1
2 cups	saltine crackers, coarsely crushed	500 mL
½ cup	crispy fried onions from Asian store	125 mL
½ cup	mayonnaise	125 mL
	Salt and pepper	
8	jumbo-jumbo, really big shrimp, peeled and deveined, tails left on	8
	Nonstick cooking spray	

Not all planks are made of wood. Try using thickly sliced pineapple as a plank. This will impart your food with a sweet flavor, and you can eat the "plank" too.

• Rinse the shrimp under cold, running water; drain and pat dry with paper towel. Take half of the shrimp and purée in a food processor. Take the other half of the shrimp and thinly slice into strips. In a bowl, combine shrimp purée and thinly sliced shrimp with green onion, red onion, red pepper, 2 Tbsp (30 mL) Southern Comfort, cilantro, sambal olek, rice vinegar, lime juice, olive oil, ginger and fish sauce. Mix well, cover and refrigerate, allowing the shrimp to marinate for 30 minutes to 1 hour.

• Meanwhile, slice the pineapple into eight ¾-inch (2 cm) thick rounds and arrange them, evenly spaced, on a plastic-lined cookie sheet. Place in freezer for 1 hour.

• Remove shrimp mixture from refrigerator and drain off any excess liquid. Add diced, room temperature pineapple, crackers, crispy fried onion pieces and mayonnaise. Season with salt and pepper and mix to combine. This shrimp mixture should be moist and sticky but not wet. When pressed together it should clump.

• Using the Cajun injector, inject the jumbo-jumbo, really big shrimp with an equal amount of the remaining Southern Comfort. Portion the chopped shrimp mixture into 8 equal-sized balls.

• Take a ball of shrimp and carefully mold it around one of the Southern Comfort-injected shrimp, leaving the tail portion sticking out of the top. Re-form the shrimp ball, pressing the mixture around the whole shrimp. Place the encased shrimp on a plastic-lined tray; cover and refrigerate for 1 hour to allow to set.

• Preheat grill to medium-high heat. Remove pineapple "planks" from freezer. Remove shrimp from refrigerator and spray each one lightly with nonstick cooking spray.

• Place one shrimp on the center of each pineapple "plank." Place pineapple planks on grill and close lid. Plank grill for 20 to 25 minutes, checking periodically to ensure your planks are not burning, until the shrimp coatings are fully cooked and the whole shrimp are opaque. Remove from grill and serve immediately.

SERVES 8

TIP: To ensure you've added enough salt and pepper to the shrimp mixture, cook a spoonful of the mixture in the microwave; taste and then add more salt and pepper if necessary to the raw ingredients.

*See (p. 192) for more information about Cajun injectors.

CEDAR-PLANKED STUFFED MUSHROOMS

1	regular plank, 15-inch (38 cm)	1
6 oz	fresh shrimp, peeled and deveined	175 g
1 Tbsp	olive oil	15 mL
½ cup	chopped onion	125 mL
3	large cloves garlic, minced	3
¼ cup	chopped fresh basil	60 mL
½ tsp	chopped fresh rosemary	2 mL
⅔ cup	fresh bread crumbs	150 mL
½ cup	grated Parmesan cheese	125 mL
¼ cup	mayonnaise	60 mL
	Salt and pepper	
10	portobello mushrooms, stems and dark gills removed, each 2 to 2½ inches (5–7 cm) wide	10

TIP: Large portobello caps may be substituted for main dish servings or button mushrooms for appetizer servings.

Recipe courtesy of Genevieve Knox
Fire & Flavor Grilling Co.
www.fireandflavor.com

• Cut shrimp to ¼-inch (5 mm) pieces and place in medium bowl; set aside. Heat oil in a large frying pan set over medium-high heat. Add onion and garlic; sauté for 4 minutes, until onion begins to soften. Stir in fresh herbs and continue cooking for an additional minute.

• Transfer onion mixture to the bowl with the raw shrimp. Stir in bread crumbs, cheese, and mayonnaise; season filling with salt and pepper. Arrange mushroom caps, gill sides up, on a baking sheet. Lightly pack shrimp filling into each mushroom cap. Mushrooms can be prepared to this point, covered and refrigerated, for up to 6 hours.

• Preheat grill to medium heat. Place soaked plank on grill, close lid and heat for 3 minutes. Flip plank and heat second side an additional 3 minutes. Carefully arrange stuffed mushrooms on plank, close lid and cook for approximately 18 minutes, until mushrooms are fork tender and filling begins to brown. Serve hot.

MAKES 5 APPETIZER SERVINGS OR 2 TO 3 MAIN COURSE SERVINGS

FIG'N DELICIOUS FIGS

1	regular cedar plank, soaked in water	1	
8	large, ripe black mission figs	8	
2 Tbsp	honey	30 mL	
½ cup	goat cheese	125 mL	
	Freshly ground black pepper		
8	slices prosciutto	8	
Drizzle	Chambord liqueur	Drizzle	

A truly decadent appetizer! When fresh figs are in season nothing beats this recipe as your BBQ show-stopper.

• Preheat grill to medium heat. Slice the stems from the figs and cut each fig three quarters of the way through the center. Drizzle the inside of each fig with an equal amount of honey.

• Fill each fig with 1 Tbsp (15 mL) of goat cheese. Season with black pepper to taste. Carefully wrap each fig with one slice of prosciutto. Arrange figs evenly on plank.

• Place plank on grill and close lid. Plank bake for 15 to 20 minutes, until the prosciutto is slightly crisp, the cheese is warm and the figs are tender and hot. Carefully remove from the grill and drizzle with a little Chambord.

SERVES 8

SWEET AND SPICY CHICKEN WINGS

1	24-inch (60 cm) regular cedar plank, soaked in water	1
5 lb	chicken wings, tips attached	2.5 kg
2	bottles Sleeman Original Draught	2
½ cup	Sweet Spice Rub (p. 48)	125 mL
½ cup	icing sugar	125 mL
½ cup	Sriracha hot chili sauce	125 mL
½ cup	Ted Reader's World Famous BBQ Crazy Canuck Sticky Chicken and Rib Sauce or	125 mL
	your favorite gourmet-style BBQ sauce	
	Sleeman Honey Brown Lager	

• Place wings in a large bowl and top with beer. Cover and refrigerate for 4 to 6 hours or overnight. Drain wings and pat dry to remove excess liquid. Toss wings with Sweet Spice Rub to coat evenly.

• Preheat grill to medium heat. Arrange seasoned wings in an even layer on plank. Place plank on grill and close lid. Cook for 30 minutes, until wings are fully cooked.

• Meanwhile, combine icing sugar, Sriracha hot chili sauce and barbecue sauce. Toss the cooked wings with sugar mixture until evenly coated. Transfer to a serving platter and serve immediately with ice-cold Sleeman Original Draught and plenty of napkins.

SERVES 4

TEQUILA LIME CHICKEN SATAY
ON VERTICAL PLANK

1	Vertical Plank (p. 40), soaked in water	1	
18	10-inch (25 cm) hardwood skewers, soaked in water for a minimum of 1 hour	18	
2¼ lb	boneless, skinless chicken breasts, thinly sliced into strips, about 2 oz (60 g) each	1.1 kg	
½ cup	El Jimador Tequila	125 mL	
½ cup	lime juice	125 mL	
¼ cup	honey	60 mL	
¼ cup	Ted Reader's World Famous BBQ Crazy Canuck Sticky Chicken and Rib Sauce or your favorite gourmet-style BBQ sauce	60 mL	
2 Tbsp	Bone Dust BBQ Seasoning (p. 46)	30 mL	
2 Tbsp	chopped fresh cilantro	30 mL	
2 Tbsp	olive oil	30 mL	
2 tsp	chipotle chili paste	10 mL	

• Thread strips of chicken onto skewers leaving at least a 2-inch (5 cm) space from the end of the meat to the point of the skewer. Place skewers into a large glass dish; set aside.

• In a bowl, combine tequila, lime juice, honey, barbecue sauce, Bone Dust BBQ Seasoning, cilantro, olive oil and chipotle chili. Whisk until well incorporated and pour three-quarters of the mixture over chicken skewers, turning to coat evenly. Reserve the remaining marinade mixture for basting during planking. Cover and refrigerate for 2 to 4 hours.

• Preheat grill to medium-high heat. Remove chicken skewers from marinade, discarding leftover marinade.

• Insert chicken skewers, pointy side down, into the drilled holes in the Vertical Plank. Push firmly to ensure that all the skewers are standing straight up.

• Place vertical planked chicken skewers onto grill and close lid. Plank for 15 to 20 minutes, checking periodically and basting with remaining tequila mixture, until skewers are just cooked through. Carefully remove from grill and serve immediately.

MAKES 18 SKEWERS

BRYN'S GRILLED CHICKEN NACHOS

1	24-inch (60 cm) cedar plank, soaked in water	1
1	small red pepper, cut in half, seeds and stem removed	1
1	small red onion, peeled and cut into ½-inch (1 cm) rounds	1
1 Tbsp	olive oil	15 mL
	Salt and pepper to taste	
3 Tbsp	sliced green olives	45 mL
2 Tbsp	chopped fresh cilantro	30 mL
3	jalapeno peppers, thinly sliced	3
2	green onions, thinly sliced	2
1 lb	boneless skinless chicken breasts	500 g
2 Tbsp	Bone Dust Seasoning (p. 46)	30 mL
1	bag nacho or tortilla chips	1
2 cups	shredded Monterey jack cheese or pepper jack cheese	500 mL
1 cup	cheddar cheese curds	250 mL
	Fire roasted jalapeno drizzle (see below)	

Bryn is one of my new cooks and he loves to make nachos. So we put them to the plank test and the nachos were yummy. We bought fresh corn tortillas, cut them into wedges and fried them in canola oil until golden brown and crisp, but feel free to use your favorite store-bought brand.

• Preheat grill to medium-high heat. Toss the peppers and onions in the olive oil and season with salt and pepper. Grill for 6 to 8 minutes, until lightly charred and tender. Remove vegetables from grill; set aside. Dice the roasted peppers and red onions; place in a bowl. Mix in the olives, cilantro, jalapenos and green onions; set aside.

• Coat the chicken in the Bone Dust Seasoning. Grill for 10 to 12 minutes until fully cooked. Remove from grill and allow to cool. Slice the grilled chicken into thin strips.

• Place the plank on a flat surface. Arrange half the nacho chips in an even layer on the plank. Scatter half the vegetable mixture and sliced chicken evenly over the nachos. Cover with half of the cheese. Repeat layers once and top with cheese curds.

• Place plank on grill and close lid. Grill for 12 to 15 minutes, until the cheese is melted throughout. Drizzle with Fire Roasted Jalapeno Drizzle and serve immediately.

SERVES 8

FIRE ROASTED JALAPENO CILANTRO DRIZZLE

4	jalapeno peppers	4
½	bunch fresh cilantro, chopped	½
3	cloves garlic, chopped	3
2	limes, juiced	2
¼ cup	olive oil	60 mL
	Salt and pepper to taste	

• Preheat grill to medium heat. Fire roast jalapeno peppers for 10 to 12 minutes, until lightly charred and tender. Remove from grill and coarsely chop.

• In a food processor, combine fire roasted jalapenos, cilantro, garlic, lime juice and olive oil. Blend until smooth. Season to taste with salt and pepper.

MAKES APPROXIMATELY 1 CUP (250 ML)

PLANKED BRIE
WITH PEACHES AND BLUEBERRIES

1	thin cedar plank (approx. 6-inch/15 cm square), soaked in water	1
1	ripe peach, thinly sliced into strips	1
½ pint	fresh blueberries	250 mL
2 Tbsp	honey	30 mL
1 tsp	chopped fresh thyme	5 mL
	Black pepper	
1	wheel Brie cheese, about 5 oz (15 g)	1
1	baguette, sliced	1

This recipe rocks! Planking soft and semi-soft cheeses is dead easy and people will go crazy for it. The rind on the cheese turns a golden color from the smoke and the cheese oozes once the rind is broken. Serve planked cheese with grilled baguette and crackers.

• Preheat grill to medium heat. In a small bowl, gently combine peach slices, blueberries, honey, thyme and season with black pepper to taste.

• Place Brie on plank and top with peach mixture. Place plank on grill and close lid. Plank grill cheese for 15 to 18 minutes, until cheese is golden brown and slightly puffy. Remove plank from grill and allow cheese to cool for 1 to 2 minutes.

• Serve immediately with sliced baguette, a few big spoons, and lots of napkins!

SERVES 4

GRAPE LEAF–WRAPPED PLANKED GOAT CHEESE

1	6-inch (15 cm) square regular cedar plank, soaked in water	1
8 oz	goat cheese	250 g
¼ cup	diced grilled red onion slices	60 mL
¼ cup	grill-roasted red pepper	60 mL
¼ cup	grilled and sliced mushrooms	60 mL
4	cloves plank-roasted garlic (see Cedar Plank-Roasted Garlic Soup, p. 51)	4
1 Tbsp	olive oil	15 mL
1 tsp	balsamic vinegar	5 mL
1 tsp	chopped fresh basil	5 mL
2 Tbsp	sliced green olives	30 mL
	Salt and freshly ground black pepper to taste	
3–4	large jarred, brined grape leaves, stems snipped	3–4
1	fresh baguette, sliced	1

• Form the goat cheese into a disk, about 1½ inches (4 cm) thick and 4 inches (10 cm) in diameter. Place disk on a parchment-lined plate and place in the freezer for 20 minutes.

• Meanwhile, in a bowl, combine grilled red onion, red pepper, mushrooms, roasted garlic, olive oil, balsamic vinegar, basil and olives. Season with salt and freshly ground black pepper to taste; set aside.

• Rinse grape leaves under cold water. Pat dry. Lay grape leaves on a flat work surface. Season leaves with a little salt and black pepper. Remove goat cheese from freezer. Place frozen goat cheese in the center of the leaves. Preheat grill to medium heat.

• Roll the leaves around the goat cheese, leaving a little of the top of the cheese exposed, but ensuring the sides are fully covered. (This will allow the cheese to bake and keep from flowing over when it gets hot and gooey. It will also allow the smoke to penetrate the cheese.) Top cheese with reserved grilled vegetable mixture and place on plank.

• Place plank on grill and close lid. Plank bake cheese bundle for 15 to 20 minutes, until the cheese is hot and gooey and the topping is hot. Remove from grill and serve immediately with sliced fresh baguette.

SERVES 4

2-FOOT PLANK PIZZA

1	24-inch (60 cm) regular cedar, maple or oak plank, soaked in water	1
1	rolling pin	1

SPICY TOMATO SAUCE:

2 Tbsp	olive oil	30 mL
½	small white onion, finely diced	½
2	cloves garlic, minced	2
1–2	hot chili peppers, minced	1–2
1	19 oz (540 mL) can plum tomatoes, crushed	1
1 Tbsp	chopped fresh oregano	15 mL
	Salt and coarsely ground black pepper	

THE CRUST:

2 cups	all-purpose flour	500 mL
¼ cup	grated Parmesan cheese	60 mL
1 Tbsp	Bone Dust BBQ Seasoning (p. 46)	15 mL
2½ tsp	baking powder	12 mL
¼ cup	cold butter, diced	60 mL
½–⅔ cup	milk	125–150 mL
¼ cup	olive oil	60 mL
2–3 Tbsp	corn meal	30–45 mL

THE TOPPINGS:

1	medium red onion, sliced into rings	1
2 Tbsp	olive oil	30 mL
	Salt and coarsely ground black pepper	
12	grape tomatoes, halved	12
1	ball (200 g) fresh buffalo mozzarella cheese, thinly sliced	1
4 oz	spicy Italian soppresatta, thinly sliced	125 g
½ cup	fresh basil leaves	125 mL

SPICY TOMATO SAUCE: In a small saucepan set over medium heat, warm the olive oil. Add diced onion, garlic and chili to pan and sauté until tender, about 2 to 3 minutes. Add plum tomatoes and oregano and bring mixture to a low boil, reduce heat to low and simmer for 15 minutes, stirring occasionally to keep from scorching. Season with salt and freshly ground pepper to taste. Remove from heat and set aside to cool. When spicy tomato sauce has cooled, add chopped fresh basil.

THE CRUST: Meanwhile, prepare the pizza dough. In a large bowl, stir together all-purpose flour, Parmesan cheese, Bone Dust BBQ Seasoning and baking powder. Add cold butter to flour mixture. Using your fingertips, rub butter and flour together until mixture resembles coarse bread crumbs. Stir in enough milk to form a ball of dough. Turn dough out onto a lightly floured surface and knead for 6 to 8 minutes or until dough is smooth and elastic. Wrap dough in plastic wrap and allow to rest for about 30 minutes at room temperature.

• Meanwhile, preheat grill to medium heat. Toss red onions with olive oil and season with salt and freshly ground black pepper to taste. Place onions onto grill and cook, turning occasionally, until lightly charred and tender, about 6 to 8 minutes. Remove from grill and slice into ¼-inch (5 mm) thick slices.

• Place dough ball onto a floured surface, and flatten slightly. Roll into a long tube, about 12 inches (30 cm) long. Using rolling pin, flatten out dough into a crust just 2 inches shorter than the length of the board, and about ¼ inch (5 mm) thick.

• Sprinkle plank with cornmeal. Lay pizza dough onto plank and brush lightly with olive oil. Place plank on grill and close lid. Plank bake crust for about 8 to 10 minutes, until top is light golden brown and the dough is just starting to get a little crisp. Open lid of grill and carefully flip pizza dough over directly on the plank.

THE TOPPINGS: Top pizza with about ¾ cup (175 mL) of tomato sauce, sliced fresh buffalo mozzarella cheese, grilled onions, sliced soprasetta, and grape tomatoes. Place plank back into grill and plank bake pizza for 6 to 8 minutes, until cheese is melted and golden, crust is golden brown, and toppings are hot.

• Garnish with fresh basil leaves and remove plank from grill and allow to cool for 1 to 2 minutes. Slice pizza into wedges and serve immediately.

SERVES 4 TO 6

BEEF SPEDINI
ON VERTICAL PLANK

1	Vertical Plank (p. 40), soaked in water	1
18	10-inch (25 cm) hardwood skewers, soaked in water for a minimum of 1 hour	18
2¼ lb	beef sirloin, thinly sliced into strips, each about 2 oz (60 g) each	1.1 kg
8	cloves garlic, minced	8
1	bottle Sleeman Original Dark Ale	1
½ cup	oyster sauce	125 mL
2 Tbsp	Sweet Spice Rub (p. 48)	30 mL
2 Tbsp	olive oil	30 mL
1 Tbsp	chopped fresh thyme	15 mL
1 Tbsp	prepared horseradish	15 mL

• Thread strips of beef onto skewers, leaving at least a 2-inch (5 cm) space from the end of the meat to the point of the skewer. Place skewers into a large glass dish; set aside.

• In a bowl, blend the garlic with the beer, oyster sauce, Sweet Spice Rub, oil, thyme and horseradish. Whisk until well incorporated and pour three-quarters of the mixture over beef skewers, turning to coat evenly. Reserve the remaining marinade mixture for basting during planking. Cover and refrigerate skewers for 2 to 4 hours.

• Preheat grill to medium-high heat. Remove beef skewers from marinade, discarding leftover marinade.

• Insert beef skewers, pointy side down, into the drilled holes in the Vertical Plank. Push firmly to ensure that all the skewers are standing straight up.

• Place vertical planked beef skewers onto grill and close lid. Plank for 15 to 20 minutes, basting periodically with remaining oyster sauce mixture, until skewers are just cooked through. Carefully remove plank from grill and serve skewers immediately.

MAKES 18 SKEWERS

PLANK CHILI GRILL STUFFED JALAPENO PEPPERS

1	Chili Pepper Grill Plank (p. 42), soaked in water	1
24	jalapeno peppers	24
8	thick slices Smoky Plank Bacon (p. 207) or store-bought double-smoked bacon, diced	8
1	small red onion, finely diced	1
1 cup	brick-style cream cheese, softened	250 mL
1	lime, juiced	1
1	green onion, minced	1
2 cups	grated orange Cheddar cheese	500 mL
1 Tbsp	chopped fresh cilantro	15 mL
2 tsp	Bone Dust BBQ Seasoning (p. 46)	10 mL
Big splash	El Jimidor Tequila	Big splash

When buying jalapeno peppers, pick out the big, long, tapered, firm peppers. These peppers will hold the most filling, fit in the plank properly and hold up to the heat of the grill.

• Wash jalapenos under cold, running water; pat dry with paper towel. Cut the tops off each jalapeno, about a ¼ inch (5 mm) down from the stem, reserving the top to use later as a cap.

• Using a paring knife or apple corer, remove the seeds and veins from peppers. Give peppers a pat on the bottom to remove all the seeds; discard seeds and veins and set clean peppers aside.

• In a frying pan, sauté the diced bacon for 3 to 4 minutes, stirring occasionally, until the bacon is getting a little crisp. Add the onion and cook for another minute until tender. Remove from heat and drain to remove excess fat. Cool.

• In a bowl, combine cooked bacon mixture, cream cheese, lime juice, green onion, Cheddar cheese, cilantro and Bone Dust BBQ Seasoning. Add a big splash of tequila and blend well. Stuff each jalapeno pepper with the bacon mixture, making sure to tightly pack the mixture into the peppers.

• Top each pepper with a reserved pepper cap. Place one pepper into each hole in the Chili Pepper Grill Plank. If the peppers are a little small, skewer with a toothpick through the center to prevent pepper from falling through the hole.

• Preheat grill to medium-high heat. Place plank on grill and close lid. Plank roast the stuffed peppers for 20 to 30 minutes, until the peppers are tender and lightly charred on the bottom and the stuffing is hot and gooey. Remove from grill and serve immediately with shots of chilled tequila.

MAKES 24 PEPPERS

TIPS:

1. Be creative with the stuffing mixture: Replace the bacon with crabmeat, shrimp, cooked ground beef or pork, grilled mushrooms and more!

2. I use a zip top plastic bag to pipe the filling into each pepper. Simply fill the bag with the bacon mixture and cut a corner off to use as a piping bag.

FISH AND SEAFOOD

MY ORIGINAL CEDAR-PLANKED SALMON

1	medium cedar plank, soaked in water	1
4	skinless Atlantic salmon fillets, 6 oz (175 g) each	4
2 Tbsp	Bone Dust BBQ Seasoning (p. 46)	30 mL
2	cloves garlic, minced	2
2	green onions, finely chopped	2
2	lemons	2
1 cup	chopped fresh dill	250 mL
½ cup	chopped shallots	125 mL
2 Tbsp	Seafood Plank Seasoning (p. 45)	30 mL
2 Tbsp	olive oil	30 mL
	Sea salt	

This should be the first recipe every new planker starts with; it's simple, impressive and delicious. Once you go smoke, you'll never go back.

• Preheat grill to medium-high heat. Season salmon fillets with Bone Dust BBQ Seasoning; set aside. Mix together the garlic, green onions, the juice of 1 lemon, dill, shallots, Seafood Plank Seasoning, olive oil and salt to taste. Spread the dill mixture evenly over the salmon fillets.

• Season plank with additional sea salt. Place plank on grill and close lid. Heat the plank for 3 to 5 minutes, until it starts to crackle and smoke.

• Open lid and place the salmon fillets on the plank. Close the lid and plank grill for 12 to 15 minutes, until cooked to medium doneness or until salmon flakes slightly when pressed. Remove plank from grill and cool for 1 minute. Squeeze remaining lemon over salmon fillets before serving.

SERVES 4

PEANUT BUTTER AND JELLY . . . FISH (SALMON)

1	24-inch (60 cm) regular plank, soaked in water	1
1	side boneless, skinless fresh Atlantic salmon, about 3 lb (1.5 kg)	1
2 Tbsp	Sweet Spice Rub (p. 48)	30 mL
3 to 5 Tbsp	smooth peanut butter, at room temperature	45 to 75 mL
3 to 5 Tbsp	pineapple preserves or Ted Reader's World Famous BBQ Pineapple Rum Sauce	45 to 75 mL
1 cup	chopped fresh pineapple	250 mL
2 Tbsp	chopped fresh dill	30 mL

I know, I know it sounds crazy and it probably is but trust me . . . it's one of the best recipes I've ever created!

• Preheat grill to high heat. Lay salmon, skin side down, on plank. Season salmon with Sweet Spice Rub and firmly press the spice rub into the flesh so that it adheres. Spread the peanut butter, using as much as necessary, to cover evenly the entire surface of the salmon.

• Stir 1 Tbsp (15 mL) of water into the pineapple preserves to thin to a spreadable consistency. Spread preserves, using as much as necessary, to cover evenly the peanut butter layer on the salmon. Sprinkle evenly with chopped fresh pineapple and dill.

• Place plank on grill and close lid. Plank bake salmon for 15 to 20 minutes, until cooked to medium doneness or until salmon flakes slightly when pressed. Peanut butter should be soft and the pineapple preserves bubbling and lightly caramelized.

SERVES 4 TO 6

PLANKED SALMON PINWHEELS
WITH LOBSTER STUFFING

2	regular cedar planks, soaked in water	2
2	cloves garlic, minced	2
½	medium red onion, finely chopped	½
1 cup	cooked lobster, coarsely chopped	250 mL
1 cup	cooked baby shrimp	250 mL
¾ cup	softened cream cheese	175 mL
½ cup	shredded mozzarella cheese	125 mL
¼ cup	coarsely chopped fresh dill	60 mL
2 Tbsp	bread crumbs	30 mL
Drizzle	oil	Drizzle
Pinch	salt	Pinch
1	boneless, skinless, center cut fillet of salmon, pin bones removed and squared, about 1½–2 lb (750 g–1 kg)	1
½	lemon	½

• In a large bowl, combine the garlic, red onion, lobster, shrimp, cream cheese, mozzarella cheese, dill, bread crumbs, oil and salt. Mix ingredients to thoroughly combine; set aside.

• With a knife, slice down the squared side of salmon, cutting three-quarters of the way through to butterfly. Open the salmon like a book to lay flat. Spread the cream cheese mixture evenly over the bottom half of the butterflied salmon into an even layer about ½-inch (1 cm) thick.

• Beginning at the bottom, roll the salmon into a pinwheel. Wrap tightly with plastic wrap; transfer to a plate and refrigerate for 1 to 2 hours to allow the fish and filling to firm up.

• Preheat grill to high heat. Transfer the salmon roll to a cutting surface. Cut the salmon roll, using a serrated knife, into 1½-inch (4 cm) to 2-inch (5 cm) pinwheels; arrange 3 to 4 slices on each plank.

• Place planks on grill and close lid. Plank bake for 20 to 25 minutes until cooked to medium, being careful not to open the lid during grilling.

REMEMBER: There is no need to turn the salmon.

• Squeeze the juice of half a lemon over the planked salmon pinwheels before removing from grill.

SERVES 6

GREAT CANADIAN CEDAR WRAP

4	8-inch (20 cm) long x 6-inch (15 cm) wide cedar wood wraps, soaked in water	4
8	6-inch (15 cm) pieces of butcher's twine, soaked in water	8
	Fresh cut cedar bows, soaked in water (optional)	
4	boneless, skinless fillets of Atlantic salmon, about 4 oz (125 g) each	4
2 Tbsp	Seafood Plank Seasoning (p. 45)	30 mL
2	green onions, minced	2
¼ cup	thinly sliced red onion	60 mL
¼ cup	thinly sliced yellow pepper	60 mL
1 Tbsp	chopped fresh dill	15 mL
1 Tbsp	olive oil	15 mL
1 Tbsp	lemon juice	15 mL
1 cup	cooked lobster meat (if using frozen lobster meat, be sure to squeeze out excess moisture)	250 mL
2 Tbsp	melted butter	30 mL

Wraps are a new trend in BBQ cooking. Thin sheets of wood are soaked and then wrapped around fish and other meats. Soak it. Roll it. Grill it.

• Season salmon fillets all over with Seafood Plank Seasoning, rubbing the seasoning into the meat; set aside. In a bowl, combine green onions, red onion, yellow pepper, dill, olive oil and lemon juice; set aside.

• In a separate bowl, combine lobster meat and melted butter, mix well to coat the lobster with the butter; set aside.

• Remove cedar wrap from water and pat dry with paper towel. Look at the wrap and see which way the grain of the wood goes. Place the salmon fillet on the cedar wrap. Top with a quarter of the onion mixture and a quarter of the lobster mixture. Following the grain of the wood, roll salmon tightly in wrap to make a cigar-shaped roll; tie in two places with the wet twine. **NOTE:** You may need someone to assist you with this part. Repeat with remaining ingredients.

• Preheat grill to medium to medium-low heat. Place soaked cedar bows on the grill (if using). Place wrapped salmon bundles on top of the cedar bows. Close grill lid and cook for 20 to 25 minutes, until the fish is just cooked through. Check grill periodically to ensure the cedar bows and wraps have not caught fire. Remove from grill. Cut twine and fold back the wrap. Serve on wrap.

SERVES 4

TIPS:

1. It is necessary to roll the wraps with the grain of the wood so that the wraps do not split. Make sure the wraps have been soaked long enough to prevent splitting.

2. Soaking the string prevents it from burning.

PLANKED SALMON
WITH SHRIMP AND TROPICAL SALSA

1	regular cedar plank, soaked in water	1
4	skinless Atlantic salmon fillets, 6 oz (175 g) each	4
1 Tbsp	Seafood Plank Seasoning (p. 45)	15 mL
4	jumbo shrimp, peeled and deveined, tails on, 4/6 per pound	4
2	sprigs cilantro	2
1	green onion, minced	1
1	Scotch bonnet or habanero chili pepper, minced	1
1	lime, juiced	1
1 cup	Lindemans Bin 65 Chardonnay	250 mL
½ cup	each orange and pineapple juice	125 mL
2 Tbsp	olive oil	30 mL
1 Tbsp	minced ginger	15 mL
	Sea salt	
½	orange	½
2 Tbsp	Tropical Salsa (recipe follows)	30 mL

TROPICAL SALSA:

1	ripe mango, diced	1
1	Cubanelle pepper, diced	1
1	red hot chili pepper, seeded and diced	1
½	small red onion, diced	½
1 cup	diced ripe persimmon, papaya, pineapple, or other tropical fruit	250 mL
1–2	passion fruit	1–2
½	orange, juiced	½
2 Tbsp	olive oil	30 mL
1–2 Tbsp	chopped fresh cilantro	15–30 mL
	Salt and freshly ground black pepper	

• Evenly space salmon fillets and shrimp in a glass dish. In a bowl, combine the cilantro, green onion, Scotch bonnet, lime juice, Chardonnay, orange juice, pineapple juice, oil, Seafood Plank Seasoning, ginger and salt to taste. Pour wine mixture over salmon and shrimp, turning food to coat evenly. Cover and refrigerate for 30 minutes.

• Preheat grill to medium-high heat. Remove salmon fillets and shrimp from marinade. Press Seafood Plank Seasoning into the salmon and shrimp; set aside.

• Season plank with sea salt, place on grill, and close lid. Heat plank for 3 to 5 minutes until it starts to crackle and smoke. Open lid and place the salmon fillets on the plank; top each salmon fillet with one shrimp.

• Close the lid and plank grill for 15 to 18 minutes until salmon flakes lightly when pressed and the shrimp are opaque and fully cooked.

• Squeeze the half-orange over salmon fillets and shrimp. Remove shrimp from top of salmon fillet; top each fillet with 2 Tbsp (30 mL) of Tropical Salsa and replace shrimp.

• Serve with chilled glasses of Lindemans Bin 65 Chardonnay.

SERVES 4

TROPICAL SALSA: In a bowl, combine mango, Cubanelle pepper, chili pepper, red onion and persimmon. Cut the passion fruit in half and scoop seeds into the mango mixture. Add orange juice, olive oil and cilantro. Season with salt and pepper to taste. Mix well to combine.

MAKES 3 CUPS (750 ML)

EGGS AND SALMON HAIDA

1	regular cedar plank, soaked in water	1
2 cups	water	500 mL
2 Tbsp	Seafood Plank Seasoning (p. 45)	30 mL
1 Tbsp	light brown sugar	15 mL
4	skinless Atlantic salmon fillets or salmon steaks, 4 oz (125 g) each	4
1	bunch Swiss chard leaves	1
2	green onions, finely chopped	2
½ cup	cream cheese, softened	125 mL
¼ cup	chopped shallots	60 mL
1 Tbsp	chopped fresh dill	15 mL
1 tsp	sea salt	5 mL

HOLLANDAISE SAUCE:

4	black peppercorns	4
1	sprig thyme	1
1	small shallot, diced	1
½ cup + 3 Tbsp	hard apple cider	25 mL + 145 mL
2 Tbsp	cider vinegar	30 mL
4	large egg yolks	4
1¼ cups	clarified butter	310 mL
1 Tbsp	Seafood Plank Seasoning (p. 45)	15 mL
1 tsp	Dijon mustard	5 mL
1 tsp	lemon juice	5 mL
Dash	hot sauce	Dash
Dash	Worcestershire sauce	Dash
	Salt and freshly ground black pepper	

EGGS:

4	large eggs	4
1 Tbsp	white vinegar	15 mL
2	English muffins, split in half	2
	water	

This **recipe** is ideal served with a glass of champagne or mimosa champagne cocktail.

• In a bowl, combine Seafood Plank Seasoning and brown sugar. Season each salmon fillet on all sides with sugar mixture; set aside.

• Wash and rinse the Swiss chard leaves several times, if necessary, to remove all sand and grit. Coarsely chop chard.

• In a large frying pan set over high heat, bring 2 cups (500 mL) of water to a boil. Season water with 1 tsp (5 mL) of sea salt and add Swiss chard. Blanch Swiss chard for 1 minute until it is tender but has not lost its vibrant color. Drain immediately into a colander and refresh under cold running water. Drain and squeeze Swiss chard to remove excess moisture.

• Transfer to a mixing bowl. Add green onions, cream cheese, shallots, dill and a dash of Seafood Plank Seasoning. Mix thoroughly. Top the salmon fillets evenly with the Swiss chard mixture. Cover and refrigerate.

HOLLANDAISE: Combine peppercorns, thyme, shallots, ½ cup (125 mL) of the hard apple cider and cider vinegar in a small saucepan and bring to a boil. Reduce the heat and simmer for 3 to 4 minutes, until the liquid has reduced by half. Remove from heat and strain, discarding solids. Let the liquid cool.

• In a medium heatproof bowl, whisk the egg yolks, remaining hard apple cider and cooled cider mixture. Place over a pot of barely simmering water and whisk constantly until the mixture is thick enough to form a ribbon when it falls from the tines of the whisk. Be careful not to turn this into scrambled eggs because then you'd be starting over. Remove from heat.

• Place the bowl with the egg mixture on a damp kitchen towel to hold it in place. While whisking constantly, slowly pour the clarified butter into the egg mixture, until all the butter has been incorporated. Season with Seafood Plank Seasoning, mustard, lemon juice, hot sauce, Worcestershire sauce, salt and pepper. Set aside and keep just above room temperature. Preheat grill to medium-high. Arrange salmon fillets on the plank. Place plank on grill and close lid. Plank bake for 15 to 18 minutes until cooked to medium doneness.

EGGS: Meanwhile, pour 4–5 inches (10–12 cm) of water into a medium saucepan. Add vinegar. Bring to a rolling boil on a stovetop burner; reduce heat so the water just simmers. Using a slotted spoon, gently stir the poaching water clockwise so that the water is swirling slightly. Crack eggs one at a time into the water. Poach eggs until the whites are set but the yolks are still soft, about 5 to 6 minutes. Using a slotted spoon, remove poached eggs from pot and drain on paper towels. Set aside, keeping warm.

• When the salmon is almost done and the plank is smoking, top each fillet with 1 poached egg. Continue to plank grill for 1 to 2 minutes just to add a little smoke flavor to the eggs.

• Remove from grill and carefully transfer each egg-topped planked salmon fillet to a toasted English muffin. Spoon over equal amounts of the hollandaise sauce and serve.

SERVES 4

COD ON A BOARD WITH BACON STRAP

2	Planks with Legs (p. 41), soaked in water	2
20	1-inch (2.5 cm) nails	20
4	fillets fresh cod, skin and tails on	4
¼ cup	Seafood Plank Seasoning, (p. 45)	60 mL
8	thick slices Smoky Plank Bacon (p. 207) cut into 4–5-inch (10–12 cm) lengths	8

My Uncle Nick (my mother's cousin) loves fish and recently sent me a letter telling me all about his new favorite, scrod. It's a saltwater fish that comes inland to fresh water to spawn. It turns out that people not only love scrod, but they love planked scrod and it's also the state fish of Connecticut. Who knew?

Finding scrod in Canada isn't that easy, though. So I called my good buddy Adam Kennedy who works for Cooke Aquaculture in Canada. It turns out that Cooke Aquaculture is now farming cod, which is a great substitute for scrod. Two days after we spoke, I received 3 whole fresh cod, weighing approximately 12 lb (5.5 kg) each (thanks, Adam!). We filleted the cod and began to plank it. This method is great, but there's nothing wrong with grilling it either. Nothing tastes better than fresh cod with bacon. Mmmmmm.

• Build a hot fire in a fire pit. When the coals are roaring and the heat is intense, it's ready to start cooking.

• Meanwhile, place one Plank with Legs on a flat surface. Place 2 fillets on each plank, lengthwise, with the tails at the end where the plank meets the legs. Fillets should be about 1 inch (2.5 cm) apart. Secure the fish to the plank by tacking a nail into the tail section. Season the cod with half the Seafood Plank Seasoning, pressing the spices gently into the flesh to adhere. Repeat with remaining plank and ingredients. Next lay 2 slices of bacon across each fillet and secure the ends to the planks with nails.

• Arrange both planks by the fire, about 12 inches (30 cm) from the hot coals. Pull the legs out and rest them on the ground like teepees. Adjust legs so that the fish sits at a 45° angle to the fire. You may need to move the fish closer to, or farther away from, the heat. The fish should be cooking evenly, but the bacon should not be scorching. Careful monitoring is required.

• Roast for 30 to 45 minutes, until the fish flakes easily from the skin and the bacon is crispy. Adjust the legs to raise the fish more upright if more heat is necessary. Using gloved hands, carefully remove the whole apparatus from the bonfire area and cool slightly before serving.

SERVES 4 TO 6

BONFIRE CANDIED SALMON

2	4-foot (1.2 m) long x 8-inch (20 cm) wide regular cedar plank	2
4	nails	4
2	sides boneless, skin on Atlantic salmon, about 3 lb (1.5 kg) each	2
½ cup	Sweet Spice Rub (p. 48)	125 mL

You will need a fire pit to prepare this recipe. The ground around the fire pit should be relatively soft, as you will need to stand the planks of salmon around the fire. Build a hot fire and when the coals are roaring and the heat is intense, you're ready to start cooking!

This is a recipe for a party—perfect for a group of people who want to have fun and can be patient for delicious, tasty salmon.

• Cut the bottom foot (30 cm) of each plank into points. (Use a circular saw to make 2 angled cuts to create the point.)

• Lay planks on a flat work surface. Place one side of salmon on each plank; position the tail section at the top, about 10 inches (25 cm) from the end of the plank. Secure the salmon to the plank by tacking a couple of nails into the tail section of the fish. (**NOTE:** The salmon won't slide off the plank because when it cooks, the fat and collagen from the skin will make it stick to the plank.) Rub the salmon liberally with the Sweet Spice Rub.

• When the fire is roaring hot and the coals are burning white, push the pointed end of the plank about 8 inches (20 cm) into the ground. The fish should be facing the fire and the plank will be leaning on a bit of an angle so that the food is about 12 inches (30 cm) from the edge of the fire.

• Grab a cold beverage; sit back and wait patiently for the salmon to cook. The fire will need to be fed occasionally by adding small logs, one at a time as the coals burn down. Try to keep the flames to a minimum by moving the logs around as needed using a poker.

• Cook the salmon for 2 to 3 hours, depending on how hot your fire is and how much wind is in the air. When fish is cooked enough to flake easily, carefully pull plank from the ground and lay on a flat surface. Serve immediately.

SERVES A CROWD

BONFIRE ARCTIC CHAR/PICKEREL ON LEGS

2	Planks with Legs (p. 41), soaked in water	2
4	1-inch (2.5 cm) nails	4
4	arctic char fillets with tails intact, 6–8 oz (175–250 g) each or pickerel fillets	4
¼ cup	Seafood Plank Seasoning (p. 45)	60 mL

Arctic Char and Pickerel are two of my favorite fish. Try this recipe with both species. Heck, we did, and it was delicious!

• Place one Plank with Legs on a flat surface. Place 2 char fillets lengthwise on the plank with the tails positioned at the same end of the plank where the nails fasten the legs of the plank. Secure the fish to the plank with 2 more nails. Evenly space the nails about 1 inch (2.5 cm) apart, and about 1 inch from end of the fish's tail. Season the char with Seafood Plank Seasoning, pressing the spices gently into the flesh to adhere. Repeat with other Plank with Legs and remaining fillets.

• Prepare the fire. Take both Plank with Legs with char to the fire. Pull the legs out and rest them on the ground like teepees. Adjust so that the fish sits at a 45° angle and place planks about 12 inches (30 cm) from the hot coals. You may need to move the fish closer to, or farther away from, the heat depending on how hot the fire is. Careful monitoring is required here to prevent the fish from scorching and the plank from igniting. Adjust the legs on the stand to raise the fish up if necessary during the cooking process to prevent scorching.

• Roast for about 30 to 45 minutes, until the fish flakes easily from the skin. Using gloved hands, carefully remove the whole apparatus from the heat and allow to cool slightly before serving.

SERVES 4

TIP: If using salmon steaks, remove bones, fold in loose ends and tie with butcher's twine to make a compact, circular-shaped piece of fish.

ON GOLDEN PLANK:
CEDAR-PLANKED RAINBOW TROUT

1	regular cedar plank, soaked in water	1
1	rainbow trout, fillet, skin on about 1 lb (500 g)	1
1	green onion, minced	1
1	lemon, peeled and segmented	1
1	lime, peeled and segmented	1
1	orange, peeled and segmented	1
1 tsp	chopped fresh dill	5 mL
Splash	Lindemans Bin 65 Chardonnay	Splash
	Sea salt and freshly ground pepper	
	Sweet Spice Rub (p. 48)	

• Preheat grill to medium-high heat.

• Season trout fillet with Sweet Spice Rub, gently rubbing the seasoning into the meat so that it adheres.

• Place trout fillet onto soaked plank. Set aside.

• In a bowl, combine green onion, lemon, lime and orange segments and dill.

• Season to taste with splash of Lindemans Bin 65 Chardonnay, sea salt, and freshly ground black pepper. Set aside.

• Place plank trout on preheated grill, close lid and grill for 15–20 minutes until fish is just cooked through.

• Remove from gill and top with citrus salsa mixture.

• Serve with Lindemans Bin 65 Chardonnay.

SERVES 2 TO 3

CILANTRO-SOY BLACK COD

1	24-inch (60 cm) regular cedar plank, soaked in water	1
1	large sweet onion, cut into 4 wedges	1
2 Tbsp	olive oil	30 mL
1	side black cod, bone removed and skin on	1
2 Tbsp	Seafood Plank Seasoning (p. 45)	30 mL
3 Tbsp	butter	45 mL
1	head plank-roasted garlic (see Cedar Plank–Roasted Garlic Soup, p. 51)	1
¼ cup	Sleeman Original Cream Ale	60 mL
1	green onion, finely chopped	1
2 Tbsp	soy sauce	30 mL
1 Tbsp	chopped fresh cilantro	15 mL
1 Tbsp	rice vinegar	15 mL

• Preheat grill to high heat. Rub onion wedges with 1 Tbsp (15 mL) of olive oil and grill for 8 to 10 minutes, until lightly charred and tender. Remove from grill and set aside to cool. Slice cooled onion into ½-inch (1 cm) thick slices; set aside.

• Place black cod, skin side down, on plank. Rub flesh of black cod with Seafood Plank Seasoning. Reduce grill heat to medium.

• Place plank on grill and close lid. Plank bake for 20 to 25 minutes, until just cooked through but still moist; the fish should flake easily with a fork.

• Meanwhile, heat a heavy bottom frying pan on the side burner of the grill. Heat remaining olive oil and 1 Tbsp (15 mL) of the butter. Add reserved onion and sauté for 1 minute, stirring constantly. Add garlic cloves; stir and deglaze the pan with beer.

• Reduce the volume of the liquid by half and add the green onion, soy sauce, cilantro and rice vinegar. Remove from heat and stir in the remaining butter; keep warm.

• When the fish is almost cooked, open grill and drizzle cod with a little bit of beer to keep it moist. Close lid and cook for another 3 minutes. Remove plank from grill. Spoon sautéed beer onions and garlic over top of planked black cod and serve immediately.

• Serve with chilled Sleeman Original Cream Ale.

SERVES 4

CEDAR-PLANKED SEA BASS
WITH CUBAN MOJITO SAUCE

2	cedar planks, soaked in water	2
¼ cup	vegetable oil	60 mL
1–2	Scotch bonnet chili peppers, diced	1–2
1	medium onion, diced	1
2 Tbsp	chopped garlic	30 mL
2	bay leaves	2
1	roasted red pepper, peeled and seeded	1
2 Tbsp	chopped fresh cilantro	30 mL
1 cup	tomato sauce	250 mL
	Sea salt and pepper	
8	2-inch (5 mL) thick skinless, sea bass fillets, 6 oz (375 g) each	8
2	limes	2

• Heat the oil in a medium saucepan set over medium-high heat. Sauté the Scotch bonnet peppers, onion and garlic for 3 to 4 minutes until tender.

• Add bay leaves, roasted red pepper and cilantro and continue to cook for 4 more minutes, stirring occasionally. Add the tomato sauce and bring the mixture to a boil. Reduce heat and simmer for 15 minutes. Season with salt and pepper to taste. Remove and discard bay leaves. Purée mixture until smooth. Adjust seasoning and cool. Mixture should be fairly thick.

• Season sea bass fillets with salt and pepper. Place sea bass in a dish; pour half of the sauce over the sea bass and marinate for 30 minutes.

• Preheat grill to high heat. Season planks with sea salt. Place planks on grill and close lid. Let the planks heat for 3 to 5 minutes until they start to crackle and smoke.

• Open lid and carefully place the marinated sea bass fillets on the planks. Close the lid and plank bake for 15 to 18 minutes until cooked to medium doneness. Periodically check that the plank is not on fire.

• While the sea bass is cooking, reheat remaining sauce. Squeeze limes over sea bass. Carefully remove the planks of sea bass from the grill and transfer to a serving platter. Serve with sauce.

SERVES 8

CINNAMON BAKED ARCTIC CHAR

24	cinnamon sticks, approximately 8 in. long	24
2 cups	Lindemans Bin 65 Chardonnay	500 mL
1	whole arctic char, 3–4 lb (1.5–2 kg) each, heads on but cleaned	1
2	shallots, peeled and sliced	2
2	sprigs fresh rosemary	2
	Sea salt and freshly ground black pepper	
	Lemon wedges	
	Spiced rum	

• Rinse char inside and out with cold water. Pat dry with paper towel and place fish into a large container. Pour wine over fish, turning to coat. Cover and refrigerate for 60 minutes, turning once.

• Preheat grill to medium heat. Remove char from fridge; discard wine. Place cinnamon stick into the cavity of the char. Add a sliced shallot and a sprig of rosemary to the fish; set aside.

• Place wine-soaked cinnamon sticks directly onto grill to form a bed. (To allow for easy removal, place cinnamon sticks on a perforated metal pizza tray, or grill tray.) Top cinnamon sticks with remaining lemon, olives and rosemary. Place stuffed char onto cinnamon stick bed. Season outside of fish with salt and pepper to taste.

• Close grill lid and bake for 30 minutes, turning once but checking occasionally to ensure that cinnamon sticks are not on fire. Fish is fully cooked when firm to the touch but flesh along the backbone flakes easily when pierced.

• Remove char from grill, and transfer directly onto a serving platter. Remove cinnamon stick from belly. Drizzle cooked fish with lemon juice and a splash of spiced rum. Serve immediately with chilled Lindemans Bin 65 Chardonnay.

SERVES 4

HOLY MACKEREL!

1	thick maple Holy Plank (p. 39), soaked in water	1
	butcher twine	
2	whole mackerel, 2–3 lb (1–1.5 kg) cleaned and scaled	2
1 cup + 2 Tbsp	Gentleman Jack Whiskey	250 mL + 30 mL
3	slices thick-sliced double-smoked bacon	3
1	leek, thinly sliced and well-washed, diced	1
	Salt and freshly ground black pepper	
	Water	
	Butter	
	Hot pepper sauce	

• Rinse mackerel inside and out with cold water. Pat dry with paper towel. Lay mackerel in a glass dish and pour over 1 cup (250 mL) of Gentleman Jack, turning to coat evenly. Cover and refrigerate for 1 hour.

• Meanwhile, in a large frying pan set over medium heat, fry bacon until crispy. Add leek to pan and sauté until soft. Remove from heat; transfer food to a large mixing bowl; cool. Add remaining Gentleman Jack and season with salt and pepper to taste. Preheat grill to medium-high heat.

• Remove mackerel from Gentleman Jack marinade, reserving liquid. Stuff cavity of mackerel with leek and bacon mixture. Tie mackerel closed with butcher's twine at 1-inch (2.5 cm) intervals.

• Place plank onto a baking tray with holes facing upward. Carefully pour water into holes in the plank and lay mackerel on one side on the plank over the holes.

• Carefully remove plank from tray, place onto grill and close lid. When wood starts to crackle, reduce heat to medium. Plank roast stuffed mackerel for 15 to 20 minutes, basting with reserved Gentleman Jack marinade occasionally until fish is fully cooked and stuffing is hot. Remove from grill; cut and remove strings and serve immediately with butter and your favorite hot sauce on the side.

SERVES 4 TO 6

WHOLE TILAPIA ROAST IN A BOX

1	Coffin (p. 37), soaked in water	1
1	whole, fresh tilapia, scaled, gutted, head intact, about 2 lb (1 kg)	1
1 Tbsp	Seafood Plank Seasoning (p. 45)	15 mL
2	cloves garlic, smashed	2
1	knob ginger (1-inch/2.5 cm), chopped	1
1	small red onion, sliced	1
1	carrot, sliced	1
½	leek, sliced and well-washed	½
¼	bunch fresh thyme sprigs	¼
1	mango, peeled and thinly sliced into half moons	1
1 cup	Lindemans Bin 85 Pinot Grigio	250 mL
2 Tbsp	butter	30 mL

• Preheat grill to medium heat. Rinse fish inside and out under cold, running water and pat dry with paper towel. Season fish inside and out with Seafood Plank Seasoning; set aside.

• Scatter garlic, ginger, red onion, carrot, leek and thyme in the base of the coffin. Lay seasoned fish on top of vegetable mixture. Lay the thinly sliced mango, overlapping each other slightly, over the fish to resemble scales of a fish.

• Pour in ¾ cup (175 mL) of wine; cover with plank box lid and place on grill. Plank roast for 45 to 60 minutes, checking periodically to ensure that the box has not caught fire.

• Meanwhile, in a small saucepan, combine remaining wine and the butter. Heat to melt butter; keep warm. When the fish is fully cooked, carefully remove from Coffin and transfer to a serving platter. Drizzle with warm wine-butter sauce. Serve immediately.

Serve with glasses of chilled Lindemans Bin 85 Pinot Grigio.

SERVES 2

GRILLED TUNA
WITH SAFFRON RISOTTO

1	regular cedar plank, soaked in water	1

SAFFRON RISOTTO:

3 Tbsp	butter	45 mL
1	small onion, finely diced	1
1 cup	arborio rice	250 mL
1 tsp	saffron	5 mL
1 cup	Lindemans Bin 65 Chardonnay	250 mL
5 cups	chicken stock	1.25 L
2 Tbsp	grated Parmesan cheese	30 mL
2 Tbsp	chopped fresh herbs such as thyme, parsley, or chervil	30 mL
	Salt and freshly ground black pepper	
2	sushi-grade tuna steaks, 2-inch (5 cm) thick, 12–16 oz (375–500 g) each	2
2 Tbsp	olive oil	30 mL
3	green onions, thinly sliced on the diagonal	3

While visiting Portland, Oregon, one of my cab drivers, an avid planker, recognized me from my television show. While we were talking food, grilling, barbecuing and planking, he told me about his planked tuna recipe. The tuna is seared on one side and then surrounded with risotto. I had never been a big fan of cooking tuna on a plank as I found it would overcook, but his enthusiasm piqued my curiosity. So, I came home and tested his recipe. He said that as far as he was concerned this was the best way to cook tuna and, to my surprise, I have to agree.

SAFFRON RISOTTO: Melt butter in a heavy saucepan set over medium heat. Add the onion and cook for 3 to 5 minutes, until tender. Add the rice and the saffron. Stir well for about 1 minute to coat the grains of rice with butter. Add the Chardonnay, stirring until most of the wine is absorbed.

• Reduce the heat to medium-low and add the chicken stock, 1 cup (250 mL) at a time; stir slowly and constantly to allow the rice to absorb the liquid before the next addition. Keep stirring for 20 to 25 minutes, until all of the stock is absorbed and the rice is creamy and tender.

• Remove from heat and stir in the Parmesan and fresh herbs. Season with salt and pepper to taste. Line a tray with foil or parchment paper and evenly spoon the risotto onto it. Cool to room temperature.

• Preheat grill to high heat. Rub the tuna steaks with olive oil, salt and pepper, gently pressing the seasoning into the meat. Place tuna steaks onto grill and sear one side for 1 to 2 minutes. Remove steaks from grill and place onto plank with grill marks facing up. Surround each steak with cooled risotto, making a 2-inch (5 cm) wall around the steaks. (Dip your hands in a small bowl of water to help keep the risotto from sticking to your hands.)

• Place the plank on the grill and close the lid. Plank grill for 15 to 18 minutes, until the internal temperature of the tuna is 130°F (54°C) for rare. Risotto should be golden brown and crisp on the outside. Remove plank from grill and allow to cool for 2 to 3 minutes. Top steaks with sliced green onion and serve immediately.

SERVES 4

CEDAR-PLANKED HALIBUT
WITH CRAB AND SCALLOP CRUST

1	regular cedar plank, soaked in water for 2 hours	1
6	boneless, skinless halibut fillets, 10–12 oz (300–375 g) each	6
¼ cup	Seafood Plank Seasoning (p. 45)	60 mL

CRAB AND SCALLOP CRUST:

3	cloves garlic, minced	3
1	bunch green onions, chopped	1
1	large red onion, finely chopped	1
1½ cups	fully cooked, chopped crab or lobster meat	375 mL
1 cup	shredded mozzarella cheese	250 mL
1 Tbsp	chopped fresh dill	15 mL
1 Tbsp	mayonnaise	15 mL
1 Tbsp	Seafood Plank Seasoning (p. 45)	15 mL
12	large sea scallops	12

• Preheat grill to high heat. Rub halibut fillets all over with Seafood Plank Seasoning, firmly pressing the spices into the meat to adhere.

CRAB AND SCALLOP CRUST: Combine garlic, green onions, red onion, crabmeat, mozzarella, dill, mayonnaise and Seafood Plank Seasoning to make the crust. Top each halibut fillet with an equal portion of the crab mixture. Arrange fillets on plank, evenly spaced.

• Using a sharp knife, slice each scallop into 4 or 5 rounds. Evenly distribute scallop rounds between fillets, creating an even layer over the crab crust. Place plank on grill and close lid. Plank grill for 12 to 15 minutes, until halibut is just cooked through and the scallops are golden.

SERVES 6

BACON-WRAPPED WHITEFISH
WITH WHITEFISH CEVICHE

1	regular hardwood maple plank, soaked in water	1
4	fresh whitefish fillets, scaled, about 8 oz (250 g) each	4
2 Tbsp	Seafood Plank Seasoning (p. 45)	30 mL
12	very thin slices double-smoked bacon, similar to the thickness of prosciutto	12
¼ cup	Finlandia Vodka	60 mL

WHITEFISH CEVICHE:

2 cups	diced whitefish fillets	500 mL
2	limes, peeled and segmented, juices reserved	2
1	green onion, thinly sliced on the bias	1
1	Thai red chili, minced	1
¼ cup	finely diced red onion	60 mL
2 Tbsp	finely diced yellow pepper	30 mL
2 Tbsp	Finlandia Vodka	30 mL
1 Tbsp	chopped fresh cilantro	15 mL
1 Tbsp	olive oil	15 mL
	Sea salt and black pepper	
	Iced vodka	

• Pat whitefish fillets dry with paper towel. Cut the fillets into 3-inch (7.5 cm) squares to make 12 pieces. Season whitefish squares with Seafood Plank Seasoning.

• Wrap each whitefish square tightly with the thinly sliced double-smoked bacon.

• Place on plank and drizzle with vodka. Allow to rest for 10 minutes while you prepare the ceviche.

CEVICHE: Combine diced whitefish with lime juice, lime segments, green onion, chili, red onion, yellow pepper, vodka, cilantro and olive oil. Season with salt and pepper to taste. Cover and refrigerate for 30 minutes.

• Preheat grill to medium heat. Place plank on grill and close lid. Plank grill for 15 to 18 minutes, until the whitefish flakes easily with a fork and the bacon is a little crisp. Remove from grill. Top each bacon-wrapped whitefish square with a spoonful of reserved whitefish ceviche. Serve immediately with iced shots of Finlandia Vodka.

SERVES 12

PLANKED GROUPER AND SHRIMP FUNDIDO

1	regular cedar plank, soaked in water	1
2	grouper fillets, 6–8 oz (175–250 g) each	2
2 Tbsp	Cajun seasoning	30 mL
2	jalapeno peppers, seeded and finely chopped	2
2	green onions, chopped	2
1	small red onion, diced	1
1	red bird's eye chili, finely chopped	1
½	red pepper, diced	½
¼ cup	chopped fresh cilantro	60 mL
¼ cup	Ted Reader's World Famous BBQ Crazy Canuck Sticky Chicken and Rib Sauce or your favorite gourmet-style barbecue sauce	60 mL
8	large shrimps, peeled and deveined, tails on, 12/15 per pound	8
2 cups	grated queso fresco or mozzarella cheese	500 mL
8	corn flour tortillas	8

• Preheat grill to high heat. Season grouper fillets with Cajun seasoning, gently pressing the seasoning into the fish to adhere; set aside.

• In a bowl, combine jalapeno peppers, green onions, red onion, bird's eye chili, red pepper and cilantro. Add barbecue sauce and mix well to combine. Add shrimp and toss to coat. Spread an equal amount of the shrimp mixture on the top of the two fish fillets.

• Place plank on grill and close lid. Heat the plank for 3 to 5 minutes, until it starts to crackle and smoke. Carefully open lid and place shrimp-topped grouper fillets on plank. Close lid and bake for 20 to 25 minutes, until cooked to medium.

• Carefully open lid, turn heat down to low and top each grouper fillet with shredded cheese. Plank bake for 2 to 3 minutes until cheese is just melted and all is ooey gooey and delicious.

• While the cheese melts, grill corn flour tortillas, turning once until lightly charred and crisp, about 1 to 2 minutes. Remove corn flour tortillas from grill. Remove Planked Grouper and Shrimp Fundido from grill and serve with grill-toasted corn flour tortillas.

SERVES 2

CEDAR-PLANKED MONKFISH
WITH CHILI-SPICED CRAWFISH CRUST

1	regular cedar plank, soaked in water for at least 4 hours	1
2	Roma tomatoes, halved lengthways	2
1	small sweet onion, quartered	1
1	large red pepper, halved and seeded	1
3 Tbsp	Cajun seasoning	45 mL
2 Tbsp	olive oil	30 mL
1 cup	crawfish tail-meat or baby shrimp	250 mL
2	cloves garlic, minced	2
2	hot chilies, minced	2
1 Tbsp	chopped fresh cilantro	15 mL
1 Tbsp	white balsamic vinegar	15 mL
	Kosher salt and cracked black pepper	
4	monkfish medallions, about 10–12 oz (300–375 g) each	4
8	slices prosciutto	8
½ cup	shaved Parmesan cheese	125 mL

I first cooked this recipe for an issue of *Bon Appétit* magazine. It is truly decadently delicious.

• Preheat grill to high heat. Season tomatoes, onion and red pepper with 1 Tbsp (15 mL) of the Cajun seasoning and toss with 1 Tbsp (15 mL) of the olive oil. Place tomatoes, onion and pepper on grill and fire-roast, turning frequently, until charred and blistered, 8 to 10 minutes. Remove from grill and cool slightly. Peel skin from tomatoes and peppers. Coarsely chop tomatoes, onions and peppers.

• In a bowl, combine chopped fire-roasted tomato, onion and pepper, crawfish, garlic, hot chilies, cilantro, white balsamic vinegar and remaining olive oil. Season with kosher salt and cracked black pepper to taste; set aside.

• Preheat grill to high heat. Season monkfish with remaining Cajun seasoning, gently pressing the spices into the fish to adhere. Wrap the circumference of each piece of monkfish in 2 slices of prosciutto and secure with a toothpick. Place prosciutto-wrapped monkfish chops onto plank.

• Spoon equal amounts of Chili-Spiced Crawfish Crust mixture on top of each monkfish chop, piling it up and pressing gently to adhere.

• Place planks on grill and close lid. Plank bake monkfish for 15 to 18 minutes, until cooked through. Garnish with Parmesan cheese.

SERVES 4

PLANKED COD
WITH CRAB AND SPINACH CRUST

2	regular cedar planks, soaked in water	2
2	boneless cod fillets, skin on, 6–8 oz (175–250 g) each	2
2 tsp	melted butter	10 mL
	Sea salt and freshly ground black pepper	

CRAB AND SPINACH CRUST:

2	shallots, finely diced	2
1 cup	cream cheese, softened	250 mL
½ cup	frozen spinach, chopped; thawed, drained and squeezed of excess moisture	125 mL
¼ cup	grated Parmesan cheese	60 mL
1 cup	lump crabmeat	250 mL
1/2 cup	each shredded mozzarella and Cheddar cheese	125 mL
4	lemon wedges	4

• Preheat grill to medium-high. Lay fillets on plank, skin side down. Brush each fillet with melted butter, season with sea salt and freshly ground black pepper to taste; set aside.

CRAB AND SPINACH CRUST: Place shallots, cream cheese, spinach and Parmesan cheese into a bowl and mix well. Season with sea salt and freshly ground black pepper to taste.

• Divide spinach crust evenly between fillets, gently pressing crust onto the fish to adhere. Top each fillet with ½ cup (125 mL) of crabmeat. Season with sea salt and freshly ground black pepper to taste. Top each fillet with shredded cheese.

• Place planks on grill and close lid. Plank bake for 15 to 20 minutes, until fish is fully cooked, crust is golden brown and cheese is melted. Serve immediately with lemon wedges.

SERVES 4

PLANKED CRAB CAKES
WITH SPICY HORSERADISH MAYO

1	regular red cedar plank, soaked in water	1
2 lbs	lump crabmeat, picked over to remove shells	1 kg
2	large eggs, beaten	2
2	green onions, chopped	2
1	small red onion, finely diced	1
½ cup	saltine crackers, crushed	125 mL
½ cup	mayonnaise	125 mL
3 Tbsp	Dijon mustard	45 mL
1 Tbsp	chopped fresh dill	15 mL
2 tsp	Seafood Plank Seasoning (p. 45)	10 mL
2 tsp	Worcestershire sauce	10 mL

SPICY HORSERADISH MAYO:

1 cup	mayonnaise	250 mL
½ cup	brick-style cream cheese, softened	125 mL
¼ cup	extra hot prepared horseradish	60 mL
1 tsp	hot sauce	5 mL
1 tsp	white vinegar	5 mL
	Salt and pepper to taste	

• Combine the crabmeat with the eggs, green onion, red onion, crackers, mayonnaise, mustard, dill, Seafood Plank Seasoning and Worcestershire sauce. Mix well. Form the crab mixture into cakes, each about 3–4 inches (8–10 cm) in diameter and 1 inch (2.5 cm) thick.

• Evenly space the crab cakes on the plank. Cover with plastic wrap and set in the refrigerator for 1 hour to rest.

SPICY HORSERADISH MAYO: Meanwhile, in a bowl, combine the mayonnaise, cream cheese, extra hot prepared horseradish, hot sauce and white vinegar; season with salt and pepper to taste. Transfer to a small serving bowl; cover and refrigerate until needed.

• Preheat the grill to medium-high. Place the plank on the grill and close lid. Plank bake for 12 to 15 minutes, until cooked through. Remove crab cakes from plank and serve 2 per person topped with horseradish mayo.

• Serve with Lindemans Bin 65 Chardonnay.

SERVES 8

GRILL-ROASTED CLAM PLANK BAKE

1	Coffin (p. 37), soaked in water	1
3	ears sweet corn, shucked (reserve a big handful of the husks) and cut into 2-inch (5 cm) thick rounds	3
1	bunch fresh thyme	1
36	live littleneck clams	36
1	large sweet onion, cut into 1-inch (2.5 cm) thick wedges	1
40	large fresh shrimp, about 2 lbs (1 kg), peeled and deveined but tails on, 21/25 per pound	40
3 Tbsp	Bone Dust BBQ Seasoning (p. 46)	45 mL
1	bottle Sleeman India Pale Ale	1

Serve with more chilled beer!

• Preheat grill to medium heat. Soak reserved cornhusks in water for 10 minutes. Line the bottom of the smoking box with fresh thyme. Place the clams on top of the thyme. Top the clams with the corn and onions.

• Season the shrimp with Bone Dust BBQ Seasoning. Top the corn and onions with the seasoned shrimp. Lay the reserved cornhusks over the shrimp. Pour in beer and place lid on smoking box.

• Place clam bake–filled smoking box on grill and close grill. Plank smoke for 45 to 60 minutes, until the clams are cooked (the shells will open) and the shrimp are cooked and opaque in color. Remove from grill. Open up smoking box and dig in!

SERVE 3 TO 4

TIP: Discard any unopened clams.

POULTRY

APPLE CIDER PLANK-ROASTED CHICKEN

1	regular apple wood or western red cedar Holy Plank (see p. 39), soaked in water or white wine/water mixture or apple cider	1
1	12-inch x 4–6-inch long grape vine, optional	1
1	fresh whole chicken, giblets and neck removed, 3–4 lbs (1.5–2 kg)	1
4 cups	apple cider	1 L
4 cups	cold water	1 L
½ cup	kosher salt	125 mL
¼ cup	Seafood Plank Seasoning (p. 45)	60 mL
1	green apple, cored and sliced	1
1	small onion, sliced	1
6	cloves garlic, chopped	6
2	sprigs fresh thyme	2
2	cans hard cider (approx.)	2

Brining is an easy way to add great flavor and it also makes chicken super moist. My omi would brine her chickens in a mixture of apple cider, water and salt. This is a twist on my grandmother's roast chicken.

• In a large pot or clean bucket that is large enough to hold a whole chicken, pour in the apple cider, cold water and salt. Stir to dissolve salt. Submerge chicken in the cider and water mixture. If necessary, add a little more water to cover chicken completely. Cover and refrigerate for 24 hours to brine.

• Remove chicken from cider and water mixture. Discard leftover brine. Pat chicken dry with paper towels. Rub chicken all over—inside and out—with Seafood Plank Seasoning, pressing the spices into the skin so it adheres. Fill the body cavity of the chicken with apple, onion, garlic and thyme. Tuck the legs into the flap of skin at the base of the body cavity of the chicken so it keeps the bird tight. Preheat grill to medium heat.

• Open a can of hard cider. Take a sip to make sure it's good. Take another sip to be certain. Pour the remaining cider into the reservoirs on the holy plank. Place grape vines (if using) on top of presoaked Holy Plank. Place seasoned chicken on top of vine on plank. Transfer plank to grill and close lid. Plank roast chicken for approximately 1½ hours or until it registers 180°F (82°C) when an instant-read thermometer is inserted into the thigh. Occasionally check that the plank is not on fire and that the reservoirs still have cider in them. If necessary, replenish reservoirs with additional cider to keep the chicken moist while it cooks.

• Remove plank from grill and allow chicken to rest for 5 minutes before carving. Discard ingredients in the body cavity.

SERVES 2 TO 4

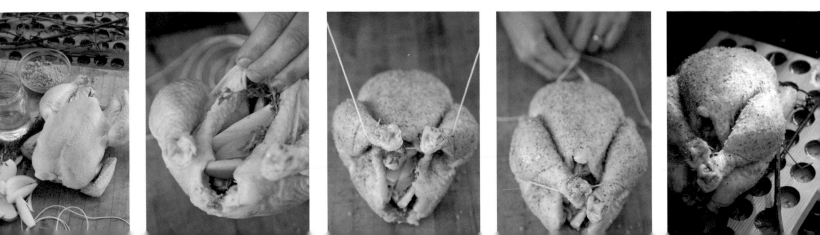

PLANK-SMOKED BEER BUTT CHICKEN
WITH HONEY BUTTER BEER BASTE

1	regular cedar plank, soaked in water	1
1	power drill	1
1	3-inch (8 cm) core drill bit hole saw blade attachment	1
1	chicken, about 4 lbs (2 kg)	1
¼ cup	Bone Dust BBQ Seasoning (p. 46)	60 mL
¼ cup	melted butter	60 mL
¼ cup	Sleeman Original Draught	60 mL
¼ cup	honey	60 mL
1	can (355 mL) Sleeman Original Draught	1

There's nothing new about beer can chicken. It's been around for so long because it produces such a moist result. The beer boils, creating steam, which makes the chicken succulent on the inside while the dry heat of the grill makes the skin nice and crispy. A new trick developed by my friend Harvey, of Bubba Q BBQ, adds a plank to the grill to create a sweet smoke flavor that makes his beer can chicken even better than the classic.

• Using the drill and the saw blade attachment, cut a 3-inch (7.5 cm) hole all the way through the center of the plank. Soak plank in water for a minimum of 1 hour.

• Preheat the grill to medium heat. Rinse the chicken inside and out with cold water and pat dry with paper towel. Rub the chicken inside and out with the Bone Dust BBQ Seasoning, massaging well and pushing some under the skin that covers the breast, directly onto the meat.

• In a small saucepan, combine butter, beer and honey. Warm slowly, stirring occasionally, until the butter is melted and mixture is warm. Set aside and keep warm.

• Open the beer and either take a big sip or pour off about 1 oz (30 mL) to make room for the liquid to boil without running over. Position the chicken, cavity down, over the can so that the can extends far enough into the cavity to hold the chicken upright.

• Place plank on grill. Place beer can in the big hole, in the plank. (The beer can should be sitting directly on the grill's grate.) Close the lid and roast for 20 minutes per pound, about 70 to 80 minutes. Baste liberally with the warm honey mixture. Chicken is fully cooked when an instant-read thermometer inserted into the thigh registers 180°F (82°C).

• Remove the chicken from the beer can very carefully using tongs and a large fork. It will be very hot and there will be steam, so lean back to protect your face. Transfer the meat to a platter and cover loosely with foil. Let rest for 10 minutes. Carve the chicken and drizzle with any extra honey mixture.

SERVES 4

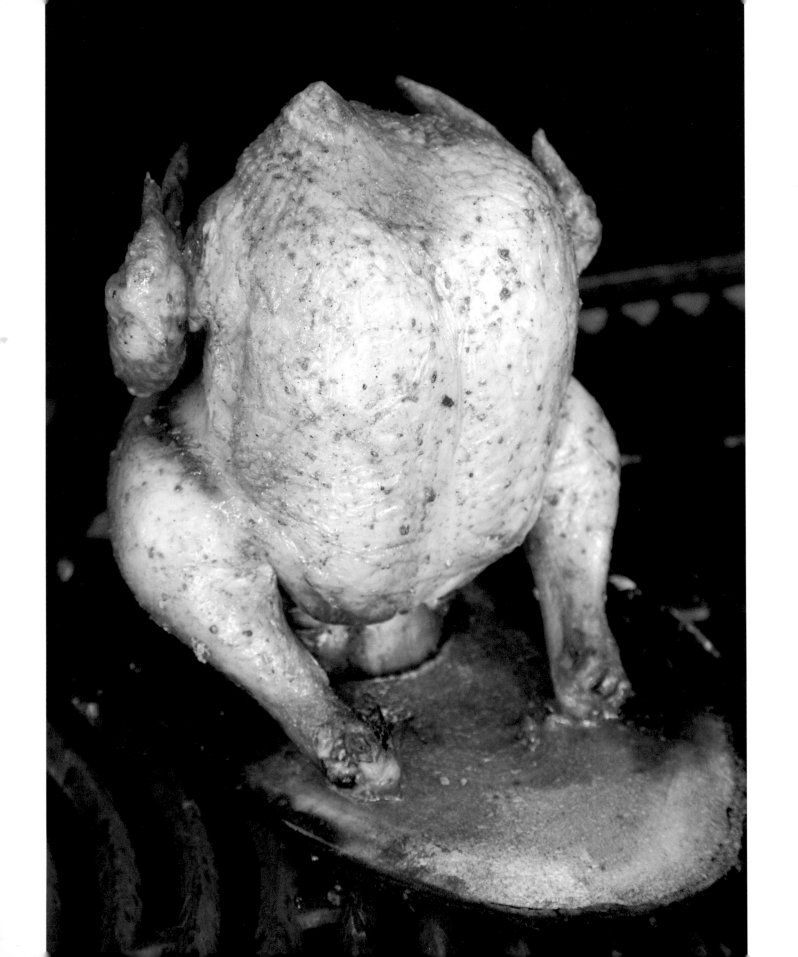

PLANK-SMOKED TURKEY
A.K.A. DEAD BIRD IN A BOX

1	Coffin (p. 37), soaked in water	1
1	turkey, 12–16 lbs (5.5–7 kg)	1
¼ cup	Seafood Plank Seasoning (p. 45)	60 mL
12	mandarin oranges, halved	12
6	heads garlic	6
4	large sweet onions, peeled, each cut into 4 wedges	4
1 cup	fresh frozen whole cranberries	250 mL
½ bunch	fresh rosemary	½ bunch

This recipe requires a grill large enough to hold the Coffin (p. 37). This is a time-consuming recipe but the results are out of this world! Try this recipe once and you'll never roast your turkey in the oven again!

• Preheat grill to medium heat. Remove giblets and neck from turkey; reserve for another use. Season the turkey inside and out with Seafood Plank Seasoning. Stuff the cavity, without packing, with as many of the mandarin orange halves, garlic, onions, cranberries, and rosemary as possible; spread any remaining ingredients evenly in the bottom of the Coffin.

• Place the stuffed turkey into the Coffin and set the two lid planks on top. You do not need to nail these down.

• Place the Coffin into the grill and close the lid. Roast for about 3½ to 4 hours (approximately 20 minutes per pound). Remove the two lid planks for the last hour to crisp and brown the skin. The turkey is ready when a thermometer inserted into the thickest part of the thigh registers 180°F (82°C).

• Carefully remove the Coffin from the grill by slipping a metal tray underneath the box (some of the nails may not be secure, depending on how burned the planks are). Allow the turkey to rest for 10 to 15 minutes and then carefully remove turkey from the Coffin to carve. Discard flavoring ingredients in and under the turkey.

• Serve with Plank Box Stuffing (p. 232).

SERVES 8 TO 12

2 HENS IN A BOX

1	medium-sized Coffin (p. 37), soaked in water	1	
	butcher twine		
2	Cornish hens	2	
3	bottles Sleeman Original Dark Ale	3	
4 cups	cold water	1 L	
¼ cup	kosher salt	60 mL	
1	lemon, halved	1	
4	shallots	4	
4	cloves garlic	4	
4	sprigs oregano	4	
2	parsnips, sliced	2	
2	carrots, sliced	2	
1	leek, sliced and well-washed	1	
1	onion, sliced	1	
	Salt and pepper		
2 Tbsp	Sweet Spice Rub (p. 48)	30 mL	

• Rinse Cornish hens under cold running water and place in a large bowl or pot large enough to hold both birds. In a second large bowl, combine 2 bottles of the beer, cold water and kosher salt. Stir to dissolve salt. Pour over Cornish hens, turning to coat evenly, cover and refrigerate for 24 hours allowing the hens to brine.

• Remove hens from brine; discard brine and rinse hens under cold, running water. Drain well and pat dry with paper towel. Stuff the cavities of each hen with lemon, shallots, garlic and oregano. Truss legs together with butcher's twine.

• In the bottom of the Coffin, place the parsnips, carrots, leek and onion. Season with salt and pepper to taste. Rub the outside of the stuffed Cornish hens with Sweet Spice Rub and place in the box. Drizzle with ½ the remaining bottle of beer. Drink remaining half bottle of beer.

• Preheat grill to medium heat. Place Coffin on grill, top with lid and close grill lid. Smoke roast hens for 60 to 90 minutes, until hens are fully cooked, juicy and tender. Cornish hens are fully cooked when an instant-read thermometer inserted into the thickest part of the thigh registers 185°F (85°).

• Remove box from grill. Rest hens for 5 minutes. Carefully remove from Coffin; cut each bird in half and serve with smoke-roasted vegetables from bottom of the smoking box.

SERVES 4

PLANKED COQ AU VIN

2	thin alder planks, soaked in water	2
1	whole chicken cut into 8 equal parts	1
3 cups	Lindemans Bin 99 Pinot Noir	750 mL
2 Tbsp	butter	30 mL
4 cups	quartered button or cremini mushrooms	1 L
2 cups	chopped Vidalia onion	500 mL
1 cup	chopped, thick-sliced, double-smoked bacon	250 mL
	Salt and freshly ground pepper	
4 cups	beef stock	1 L

Soaking the plank in red wine will infuse a sweet smoke flavor into the tender skin of the chicken breasts.

• Season chicken parts with salt and freshly ground pepper.

• Place the chicken parts into a non-reactive dish and pour over the wine, turning to coat. Cover and refrigerate for 24 hours. Remove the chicken breasts from the wine and refrigerate until needed; reserve wine.

• Melt butter in a saucepan set over medium-high heat. Add the mushrooms, onions, and bacon. Sauté for 8 to 10 minutes, stirring frequently, until lightly browned and tender. Add reserved wine from the marinade and beef stock. Bring to a boil and simmer until the volume is reduced to 3 cups (750 mL), about 30 minutes; set aside. Sauce can be kept warm or reheated when necessary.

• Preheat grill to medium heat. Evenly space the chicken breasts on the planks and place on the grill. Close the grill lid and plank roast for 20 to 25 minutes, until the chicken is crisp, golden brown and registers 180°F (82°C) on an instant-read thermometer.

• Serve each breast with a ½ cup (125 mL) of sauce.

SERVES 6

TURKEY, MUSHROOM, SPINACH, AND FETA MEAT LOAF

1	Plank Roasting Pan (p. 36), soaked in water	1
2 lbs	lean ground turkey	900 g
1½ lbs	smoked turkey, finely diced	800 g
1	small white onion, finely diced	1
3	cloves garlic, minced	3
2	green onions, finely chopped	2
1 to 2 Tbsp	fresh oregano, chopped	15 to 30 mL
2 Tbsp	Seafood Plank Seasoning (p. 45)	30 mL
1	large egg yolk	1
¼ cup	bread crumbs	60 mL
¼ cup	grated Parmesan cheese	60 mL

MUSHROOMS:

1 lb	large oyster mushrooms	500 g
½ lb	jumbo white mushrooms	250 g
¼ cup	olive oil	60 mL
2 oz	ouzo	30 mL
2 Tbsp	lemon juice	30 mL
4 tsp	Seafood Plank Seasoning, approx. (p. 45)	20 mL
1½ cups	frozen spinach, thawed, drained and squeezed of excess moisture, chopped	325 mL
1 cup	crumbled Greek feta cheese	250 mL
1 Tbsp	chopped fresh oregano	15 mL
2	cloves garlic, minced	2
1 Tbsp	olive oil	15 mL
	Tzatziki Sauce (recipe follows)	

My **sixth** visit with Regis and Kelly was the Friday before the Super Bowl. They were having a week-long Super Bowl special with a different guest chef each day and saved me, their favorite Canadian chef, for the Friday anchor. We prepared this recipe and everyone loved it; it's almost as delicious as Kelly is herself.

• In a large bowl, gently combine the ground turkey, smoked turkey, onion, garlic, green onions, oregano, Seafood Plank Seasoning, egg yolk, bread crumbs and Parmesan until evenly incorporated, about 1 minute. Cover and refrigerate for 1 hour to allow meat to rest and flavors to blend.

MUSHROOMS: Preheat grill to medium-high heat. Toss mushrooms in olive oil, ouzo and lemon juice. Season mushrooms with 1 Tbsp (15 mL) Seafood Plank Seasoning. Grill mushrooms for 6 to 8 minutes, until lightly charred and tender; cool slightly.

• Slice the white mushrooms and tear the oyster mushrooms into ½-inch (1 cm) strips. Toss mushrooms with spinach, feta, oregano and garlic. Season to taste with additional Seafood Plank Seasoning; refrigerate.

• Reduce grill temperature to medium heat. Remove turkey mixture from refrigerator and firmly press into an even layer in the Plank Roasting Pan. (Moistening hands with cold water will help keep the meat loaf mix from sticking to them.)

• Brush meat loaf lightly with olive oil. Place a foil pan between the grill and the burners to catch any meat loaf drippings. Place plank on grill directly over the foil pan. Plank roast for 45 minutes or until meat loaf registers 165°F (74°C) on an instant-read thermometer. Check plank occasionally during cooking for possible flare-ups. If necessary, reduce heat or move plank to indirect heat.

• Carefully open grill lid, allowing smoke to escape. Top meat loaf with the reserved mushroom mixture.

• Close lid and continue to cook meatloaf for 15 to 20 minutes, until meat loaf registers 185°F (85°C) on an instant-read thermometer. Remove from grill and allow meat loaf to rest for 5 minutes. Slice meat loaf into 1–2-inch (2.5–5 cm) slices and serve with Tzatziki Sauce.

SERVES 4 TO 6

TZATZIKI SAUCE:

1 cup	sour cream	250 mL
½ cup	yogurt	125 mL
½	cucumber, peeled, seeded and grated	½
3	cloves garlic, minced (approx.)	3
2 tsp	lemon juice	10 mL
½ cup	crumbled Greek feta cheese	125 mL
	Salt and freshly ground black pepper	

TZATZIKI SAUCE: In a bowl, combine sour cream, yogurt, cucumber and up to 3 cloves garlic, or to taste. Stir in the lemon juice and feta. Season mixture with salt and pepper to taste. Transfer to a small serving dish; cover and refrigerate until meat loaf is ready to serve.

MAKES APPROXIMATELY 2 CUPS (500 ML)

CINNAMON-SKEWERED HONEY GARLIC ORANGE CHICKEN THIGHS

12	boneless, skin on, chicken thighs	12
24	thin cinnamon sticks	24
6	cloves garlic, minced	6
1 Tbsp	coarsely ground black pepper	15 mL
1 tsp	coarse salt	5 mL
1 tsp	ground cinnamon	5 mL
2	oranges, zested and juiced	2
2 Tbsp	vegetable oil	30 mL

HONEY GARLIC ORANGE BBQ GLAZE:

3 Tbsp	butter	45 mL
½ tsp	ground cinnamon	2 mL
1 Tbsp	chopped fresh ginger	15 mL
2 Tbsp	chopped fresh garlic	30 mL
1 Tbsp	chopped fresh herbs, such as parsley, sage and thyme	15 mL
½ cup	honey	125 mL
¼ cup	Southern Comfort liqueur	60 mL
1 cup	orange juice	250 mL
2 Tbsp	hoisin sauce	30 mL
1 Tbsp	sesame seeds	15 mL
1 tsp	cornstarch	5 mL
2 Tbsp	cold water	30 mL
	Salt and pepper to taste	

• Skewer each chicken thigh with two cinnamon sticks. Make sure to skewer the thighs from side-to-side through the meat of the chicken and under the skin.

• In a small bowl, mix together garlic, pepper, salt and cinnamon. Rub all over the skewered chicken thighs. Place in a glass dish; stir in the orange juice, zest and vegetable oil. Cover and refrigerate for 2 hours.

HONEY GARLIC ORANGE BBQ GLAZE: Meanwhile, melt butter in a medium saucepan set over medium-high heat. Sauté the cinnamon, ginger and garlic for 2 to 3 minutes, until fragrant. Add the herbs, honey, Southern Comfort, orange juice, hoisin sauce and sesame seeds. Bring to a boil; reduce heat and simmer for 3 minutes.

• Mix together the cornstarch and water until smooth. Whisk into the sauce and return to a boil; cook, stirring, until thick. Season to taste with salt and pepper. Cool slightly. Divide in half.

• Preheat grill to medium-high heat. Remove skewered chicken thighs from orange marinade; discard the leftover marinade. Grill chicken thighs for 10 to 12 minutes or until a thermometer inserted into the thickest part of the thigh indicates 180°F (82°C). Baste frequently with half the Honey Garlic Orange BBQ Glaze during grilling. Serve with remaining sauce.

SERVES 6

CEDAR-PLANKED HONEYCOMB CHICKEN BREASTS

1	regular cedar plank, soaked in water	1
½ cup + ½ cup	honeycomb	125 mL 125 mL
½ cup	grated Romano cheese	125 mL
2 Tbsp	chopped fresh thyme	30 mL
2	green onions, roughly chopped	2
¼ cup	butter, softened	60 mL
4	boneless, skinless chicken breasts, about 6–8 oz (175–250 g) each	4

The combination of the plank and the honeycomb make this stuffed chicken breast both delicate and delicious. When you cut into the center of the chicken breast and watch the honeycomb butter ooze with sweet goodness—marvelous!

• In a bowl, using a fork, break up ½ cup of honeycomb; blend in the Romano cheese, thyme, green onions and butter to make a coarse mixture. Form the honeycomb butter into four 2-Tbsp (30 mL) balls; press to flatten. Place the honeycomb butter patties in the freezer for 1 hour. Reserve the remaining butter at room temperature.

• Lay the chicken breasts, skin side down, on a flat surface; remove the chicken tenderloins (sometimes also called the "fingers"). Lay the chicken tenderloins between 2 sheets of plastic wrap and gently pound flat; set aside.

• Using a sharp knife, cut a pocket about 1-inch (2.5 cm) deep from the top of each breast to the bottom. Using your fingers, carefully push the meat apart to make a large pocket; set aside.

• Place 1 frozen honeycomb butter portion into each chicken cavity. Place a flattened tenderloin over the cavity and tuck the tenderloin into the opening, firmly pressing the edges to make a tight seal that will keep the honeycomb butter stuffing from seeping out.

• Preheat grill to medium-high; approximately 450°F (230°C).

• Place on soaked plank. Plank bake for 30 minutes, until fully cooked, until a thermometer inserted into the thickest part of the chicken registers 180°F (82°C).

• Remove pan containing plank from the oven. Top each breast with a tablespoon of remaining honeycomb. Let rest for 5 minutes and serve immediately.

• Serve with Sleeman Honey Brown Lager or Porter.

SERVES 4

NOTE: When planking in the oven, never let the liquid run out. Check frequently and refill liquid when necessary.

LEMON CHICKEN MERINGUE PIE

2	regular cedar, oak or maple planks, soaked in water	2
	Nonstick cooking spray	

VODKA/LEMON MARINADE:

½ cup	Finlandia Vodka	125 mL
½ cup	freshly squeezed lemon juice	125 mL
2 Tbsp	olive oil	30 mL
3	garlic cloves, smashed	3
2	Thai red chilies, chopped	2
1	lemon, thinly sliced	1
1	4-inch (10 cm) piece lemon grass, smashed and thinly sliced	1
Handful	fresh cilantro chopped	Handful
4	boneless, skin on chicken breasts, about 5 oz (150 g)	4

PIE CRUST:

1	biscuit recipe, (p. 259)	1

LEMON PIE BBQ SAUCE:

½ cup	lemon curd	125 mL
½ cup	sweet Thai chili sauce	125 mL
2 Tbsp	Finlandia Vodka	30 mL

MERINGUE:

4	egg whites	4
1 tsp	cream of tartar	5 mL
½ tsp	lemon zest	2 mL

VODKA/LEMON MARINADE: In a bowl, combine the vodka, lemon juice, olive oil, garlic, chili pepper, lemon slices, lemon grass and cilantro. Evenly space chicken breasts in a glass dish and pour over marinade, turning chicken to coat evenly. Cover and refrigerate for 4 hours or overnight.

PIE CRUST: Prepare biscuit dough recipe as per instructions (page 259). Roll out dough and cut into 4 oval-shaped discs, each approximately 3-inches (7.5 cm) wide and 6-inches (15 cm) long. Each piece should be just a little bigger in size than the chicken breasts.

• Spray the plank with nonstick cooking spray. Lay dough discs, evenly spaced, on a plank, using two per plank; set aside.

• Preheat grill to medium-high heat. Remove chicken from marinade, discarding leftover marinade. Grill chicken breasts, skin side up, for 3 to 4 minutes to sear and start the chicken cooking from the bottom side.

• Remove chicken from grill and center one chicken breast on each biscuit dough disc. Place plank on grill and close lid. Plank roast chicken for 15 to 20 minutes longer, checking periodically that the plank has not caught fire.

LEMON PIE BBQ SAUCE: Meanwhile, in a bowl, combine the lemon curd, sweet Thai chili sauce and vodka. Spoon the Lemon Pie BBQ Sauce over the chicken breasts during the last 10 minutes of cooking time, close lid and continue to cook.

MERINGUE: Working quickly during the final minutes of the chicken's cooking time, prepare the meringue. In a large, very clean, grease-free stainless-steel bowl, whisk the egg whites until stiff peaks form. Gently fold in cream of tartar and lemon zest.

• When the chicken is just done, spoon large puffs of whipped egg whites over top of the lemon pie filling–basted chicken. Reduce grill heat to low and allow the meringue to brown. Remove from grill and serve immediately.

SERVES 4

TEQUILA-PLANKED CHICKEN CHILLIQUILLAS

1	Plank Roasting Pan (p. 36), soaked in water	1
	Nonstick cooking spray	
4	boneless, skinless, chicken breasts, about 6 oz (175 g) each	4
2 Tbsp	olive oil	30 mL
	Salt and pepper	
12 cups	tortilla chips, lightly broken into pieces	3 L
6 cups	Fire-Roasted Salsa (recipe follows)	1.5 L
3 cups	sour cream	750 mL
2 cups	shredded pepper jack cheese	500 mL

FIRE-ROASTED SALSA:

24	Roma tomatoes	24
2	large onions, halved	2
2	large red peppers	2
2	large yellow peppers	2
2	large Cubanelle peppers	2
1	bunch green onions	1
	A whole mess of chilies, jalapenos or serrano chilies, whatever ya got!	
1	lime, juiced	1
¼	bunch cilantro	¼
¼ cup	olive oil	60 mL
¼ cup	El Jimador Tequila	60 mL
1 Tbsp	Bone Dust BBQ Seasoning (p. 46)	15 mL

• Preheat grill to medium-high heat. Brush chicken breasts with oil and season with salt and pepper. Grill chicken, turning halfway through, for 20 minutes, until fully cooked. Remove chicken from grill and cool slightly. Using two forks, shred the chicken into thin strips; set aside.

• Spray bottom and sides of Plank Roasting Pan with nonstick cooking spray. Spoon just enough salsa into the bottom of the Plank Roasting Pan to coat evenly. Scatter 6 cups (1.5 L) of tortilla chips into the bottom of the pan.

• Sprinkle half the chicken over the chips. Cover with 3 cups (750 mL) of the salsa. Spread 1½ cups (375 mL) of sour cream over the salsa. Sprinkle 1 cup (250 mL) of shredded cheese over the sour cream. Repeat layers with remaining ingredients.

• Place pan on grill and close lid. Plank bake for 30 to 35 minutes, until smoky and the cheese on top is bubbly. Remove from grill. Rest for 10 minutes. Serve with extra Fire-Roasted Salsa, sour cream and guacamole.

• Serve with chilled shots of El Jimador Tequila.

SERVES 12

FIRE-ROASTED SALSA: Preheat grill to high heat. Fire roast the tomatoes, onions, red, yellow and Cubanelle peppers, green onions and chilies until lightly charred and tender. Place all of the charred vegetables in a large bowl and cover tightly with plastic wrap. Rest for 10 minutes.

• Remove plastic wrap from bowl and peel away the charred black skin from the peppers.

• Finely chop the peeled peppers and charred onions, tomatoes and green onions.

• Add lime juice, cilantro, oil, tequila and Bone Dust BBQ Seasoning. Stir and set aside.

MAKES APPROXIMATELY 6 TO 8 CUPS (1.5 TO 2 L)

SMOKIN' CHICKEN CIGAR WRAP

4	8-inch (20 cm) long x 6-inch (15 cm) wide cedar wood wraps, soaked in water	4
8	6-inch (15 cm) pieces of butcher's twine, soaked in water	8
¼ cup	butter	60 mL
2	medium red peppers, diced	1
1	large onion, diced	1
3	green onions, chopped	3
3 cups	cornbread, crumbled	750 mL
½ cup	shredded, smoked mozzarella cheese	125 mL
¼ cup	diced dried pear or raisins	60 mL
¼ cup	Southern Comfort liqueur	60 mL
	Salt and pepper	
4	boneless, skin on chicken legs	4
2 Tbsp	Bone Dust BBQ Seasoning (p. 46)	30 mL
4	slices bacon, fried but not crisp	4

• Preheat grill to medium-high heat. In a frying pan, melt butter. Add peppers and onion, cook for 2 to 3 minutes, until tender. Remove from heat and transfer to a bowl.

• Combine pepper mixture with green onions, cornbread, mozzarella, dried pear and liqueur. Season with salt and pepper to taste; set aside. The mixture should be moist and sticky but not wet.

• Place the chicken legs in a single layer between two sheets of plastic wrap. Using a meat mallet, pound the chicken legs so that they are uniform in thickness, about ¼–½-inch (5 mm–1 cm) thick.

• Spread a flattened chicken leg out on a flat work surface, skin side down.

• Season chicken with an equal amount of Bone Dust BBQ Seasoning. Take a quarter of the cornbread mixture and place it at one end of the flattened meat. Tightly roll the chicken around the stuffing into a cigar shape.

• Tightly wrap a strip of partially cooked bacon around each chicken roll. Repeat with remaining ingredients. Place bacon-wrapped chicken onto wraps. Following the grain of the wood, roll chicken tightly in wrap to make a cigar-shaped roll; tie in two places with the wet twine. **NOTE:** You may need someone to assist you with this part. Repeat with remaining ingredients.

• Preheat grill to medium heat. Place wraps on grill. Set the burner directly under the wraps to low heat and close lid. Wrap-roast for 25 to 30 minutes, checking periodically to ensure that the wraps have not caught fire, until an instant-read thermometer inserted into the thickest part of the wrap registers 170°F (76°C). Remove from grill and rest for 5 minutes. Cut twine, unwrap and serve immediately.

SERVES 4

PLANKED BACON-WRAPPED CHICKEN THIGHS
WITH JACK DANIEL'S BBQ SAUCE

1	regular cedar plank, soaked in water	1
8	boneless, skinless chicken thighs	8
2 Tbsp	Bone Dust BBQ Seasoning (p. 46)	30 mL
8	slices thick-sliced bacon	8
2 Tbsp	Jack Daniel's Whiskey	30 mL
½ cup	Ted Reader's World Famous Crazy Canuck Sticky Chicken and Rib BBQ Sauce or your favorite gourmet-style BBQ sauce	125 mL

• Preheat grill to medium heat. Evenly coat chicken thighs with Bone Dust BBQ Seasoning. Tightly roll the thighs up like jelly rolls, starting at the narrow end of each thigh.

• Take one slice of bacon and spread it out onto a flat work surface. Place one chicken thigh at one end on the bacon and wrap the bacon tightly around the chicken thigh. Repeat with remaining thighs. Evenly space bacon-wrapped chicken thighs on plank. Place plank on grill and close lid.

• Plank bake chicken for 15 to 30 minutes, checking occasionally to ensure that the plank is not on fire. Meanwhile, combine the Jack Daniel's with the barbecue sauce. Baste bacon-wrapped chicken thighs liberally and evenly with Jack Daniel's-flavored barbecue sauce for 10 to 15 minutes more so that the meat gets sticky and cooks through. Remove from grill and serve immediately.

SERVES 4

APPLE-JACK–STUFFED PLANKED TURKEY BREAST

1	thick hickory, oak, maple or mesquite plank, soaked in water	1
1	boneless, skin on turkey breast, about 3–4 lbs (1.5–2 kg)	1
4 cups	apple juice	1 L
2 cups	water	500 mL
1 cup	Jack Daniel's Whiskey	250 mL
¼ cup	kosher salt	60 mL

STUFFING:

4 cups	cubed, day-old, white bread	1 L
1	medium onion, diced	1
1	stalk celery, diced	1
½ cup	diced dried apricot	125 mL
¼ cup	golden raisins	60 mL
¼ cup	diced dried apple	60 mL
1 Tbsp	chopped fresh sage	15 mL
¼ cup	Seafood Plank Seasoning (p. 45)	60 mL
Big splash	Jack Daniel's Whiskey	Big splash
⅓ cup	melted butter	75 mL

• Rinse turkey breast under cold, running water and pat dry with paper towel. Using a sharp, thin-bladed knife, make a pocket in the turkey breast for the stuffing mixture. Start at the thick end of the turkey breast. Insert the tip of the knife into the thickest portion of the meat; slice down almost the entire length of the breast, stopping short about 2 inches (5 cm) from each end. Use the knife to enlarge the cavity to hold stuffing.

• Place turkey breast into a large roasting pan. In a bowl, combine apple juice, water, Jack Daniel's and kosher salt. Pour over turkey breast. Cover and refrigerate, allowing the turkey to brine for 24 hours. Turn the turkey breast a few times to ensure even brining.

STUFFING: Meanwhile, prepare the stuffing mixture. In a large bowl, combine bread cubes, onion, celery, apricots, raisins, apples, sage, 1 Tbsp (30 mL) Seafood Plank Seasoning and a big splash of Jack Daniel's. Drizzle with melted butter and mix well. The mixture should be sticky and a little wet but not mushy; set aside.

• Remove turkey breast from brine; discard brine. Pat turkey breast dry with paper towel on the outside and inside the pocket you made with the knife. Stuff the pocket with the bread stuffing, pushing firmly so it is well-packed.

• Rub the outside of the meat with remaining Seafood Plank Seasoning. Preheat grill to medium heat. Place stuffed turkey breast on plank. Place plank on grill and close lid. Plank roast for 1½ hours, until fully cooked and internal temperature of turkey reaches 170°F (77°C) with a meat thermometer, and stuffing registers 165°F (74°C). Remove from grill. Rest for 10 minutes before carving.

SERVES 6

SWINGING CHICKEN BACON-WRAPPED BBQ DRUMSTICKS

1	12-inch (30 cm) x 8-inch (20 cm) regular cedar plank, soaked in water	1
12	chicken drumsticks or thighs	12
¼ cup	Bone Dust Seasoning (p. 46)	60 mL
12	slices bacon	12
12	toothpicks	12
4	cloves garlic, minced	4
1½ cups	ketchup	375 mL
½ cup	honey	125 mL
2 Tbsp	lemon juice	30 mL
1 Tbsp	chopped fresh rosemary	15 mL
1 Tbsp	Worcestershire sauce	15 mL
	Salt and pepper	

This recipe uses a chicken leg and wing grill rack. You can find this rack in most BBQ specialty stores. It is the most efficient way to grill wings, legs and drumsticks; it allows the meat to cook evenly and it reduces flare-ups.

• Rub chicken pieces with Bone Dust Seasoning, pressing the spices evenly into the meat and skin. Roll a slice of bacon tightly around each chicken drumstick and fasten with a toothpick. In a bowl, whisk together the garlic, ketchup, honey, lemon juice, rosemary and Worcestershire sauce until combined; season sauce mixture with salt and pepper to taste.

• Preheat grill to medium heat. Hang bacon-wrapped chicken drumsticks by the knuckle (also called the joint) on the wing grill rack. Place the soaked plank on the grill. Place the rack of chicken drumsticks onto the plank. Close lid and plank roast the drumsticks for 25 to 30 minutes, basting with the ketchup mixture during the last half of cooking. Serve immediately or cool thoroughly and place in an airtight container to eat cold or to pack for a picnic.

SERVES 6

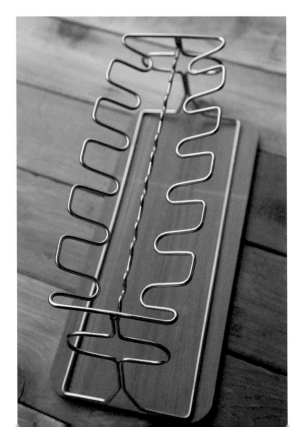

SHAKE AND BAKE CHICKEN

1	regular cedar, maple or oak plank, soaked in water	1
8	skin on, bone in chicken thighs	8
1½ cups	Japanese panko bread crumbs	375 mL
¼ cup	grated Parmesan cheese	60 mL
¼ cup	Bone Dust BBQ Seasoning (p. 46)	60 mL
	Dipping sauce	

My friend Mike Zaborsky is a *plankaholic*. He truly is my greatest fan and his addiction for planked food is immense. Thanks for this great recipe Mike! It's crispy on the outside and moist and juicy on the inside.

• Preheat grill to medium heat. Trim chicken thighs of excess fat and discard.

• Combine the bread crumbs, Parmesan cheese and Bone Dust BBQ Seasoning in a large self-sealing bag.

• Add 4 chicken thighs, seal bag and shake to evenly coat the chicken. Remove thighs and place on plank. Repeat with remaining thighs.

• Place plank on grill and close the lid. Plank roast chicken for 20 to 25 minutes, until golden brown and crisp. Remove from grill and serve immediately with your favorite dipping sauce.

SERVES 4

MEAT

PLANKED MEAT LOAF
WITH SWEET POTATO ICING

1	cedar plank, 2 feet long, 1 inch thick	1

SWEET POTATO ICING:

4	large sweet potatoes	4
¼ lb	unsalted butter (1 stick), at room temperature	125 g
3 Tbsp	brown sugar	45 mL
	Salt and pepper	

PORK MEAT LOAF:

½ cup	golden sultana raisins	125 mL
½ cup	Jack Daniel's Whiskey	125 mL
4 lb	ground pork	2 kg
6	cloves garlic, minced	6
1	large sweet onion, finely diced	1
½ cup	Japanese panko bread crumbs	125 mL
2 Tbsp	Bone Dust BBQ Seasoning (p. 46)	30 mL
¼	bunch fresh parsley, chopped	¼
3 Tbsp	grated Parmesan cheese	45 mL

TIP: When making this recipe, you need to make the Sweet Potato Icing recipe at least 4 hours in advance, and the day before is even better. The icing needs to be cold when applied to the meat loaf, or it will not stick to the meat but run off the plank onto the grill.

This is a fair bit of work but it's so worth the effort. Give it a try—you can handle it.

SWEET POTATO ICING: Preheat grill to medium heat. Place sweet potatoes onto top rack of grill; close lid and roast for 45 to 60 minutes, until flesh is soft all the way through when pierced with a fork.

• Remove sweet potatoes from grill and cool slightly. Carefully remove skin and discard (skin should be crunchy and peel off easily); ensure that no charred bits of skin are stuck to the sweet potatoes.

• Place potatoes in a large bowl and mash until smooth. Add butter and brown sugar, stirring gently to combine. Season sweet potato mixture with salt and pepper to taste; set aside to cool completely. Cover and refrigerate for 4 hours or overnight.

PORK MEAT LOAF: Soak raisins in Jack Daniel's until soft and plump. In a large bowl, combine plump raisins with the ground pork, garlic, sweet onion, panko bread crumbs, Bone Dust BBQ Seasoning and parsley.

• Place plank on a flat work surface. Form a meat loaf log that runs the entire length of the plank, leaving a 1½-inch (4 cm) border around the meat loaf to the edge of the plank. (**NOTE:** Tightly pack the meat mixture when forming the meat loaf, to ensure it will hold together and to create a nice finished texture.) Cover and refrigerate for 1 hour.

• Meanwhile, remove Sweet Potato Icing from refrigerator and warm up, at room temperature, until soft enough to spread. Stir Sweet Potato Icing to smooth out any lumps; set aside.

• Preheat grill to medium-high heat. Place planked meat loaf on the grill and close lid. Plank bake for 10 minutes. Reduce heat to medium and continue to cook meat loaf for 20 minutes. Open grill and remove planked meat loaf. Cool for 10 minutes.

• Spread Sweet Potato Icing evenly over the top and sides of the meat loaf. Use a rubber spatula to smooth the icing. (It should be approximately ½-inch (1 cm) thick all the way around the meat and there should be a 1-inch (2.5 cm) border around the plank.)

• Return plank to the grill and close lid. Continue to cook for 30 to 40 minutes longer or until an instant-read thermometer inserted into the thickest part of the meat loaf, registers 170°F (76°C). Dust with Parmesan cheese. Remove from grill. Rest for 10 minutes. Slice and serve immediately.

SERVES 8

PLANKED LONDON BROIL

1	regular cedar plank, soaked in red wine/water mixture	1
	butcher twine	
1½ lb	flank steak	750 g
1½ cups	Sleeman Fine Porter	375 mL
4	cloves garlic, minced	4
¼ cup	Dijon mustard	60 mL
2 Tbsp	fresh herbs, such as rosemary, parsley and thyme, chopped	30 mL
1 tsp	black pepper, freshly cracked	5 mL

LONDON BROIL FILLING:

1½ lb	regular ground beef	750 g
3	cloves garlic, minced	3
1	small yellow onion, diced	1
½ cup	pimento-stuffed green olives, sliced	125 mL
3 Tbsp	fresh herbs, such as rosemary, parsley and thyme, chopped	45 mL
1 Tbsp	Dijon mustard	15 mL
1 Tbsp	Bone Dust BBQ Seasoning, (p. 46)	15 mL
1 tsp	salt	5 mL
dash or 2 each	Worcestershire sauce and hot sauce	dash or 2
1 cup	Fire-Roasted Hickory-Planked BBQ Sauce (p. 227)	250 mL

Ask your butcher to butterfly the flank steak for you; it will save you time and you don't have to pay for it if they make a mistake! You can also buy fresh, store-prepared London broil and just simply plank it.

• Using a sharp knife, trim any excess fat and sinew from the flank steak. Butterfly the flank steak by slicing horizontally almost through the middle of the narrow side of the flank. Unfold the flank steak to make a rectangle or square, about ½-inch (1 cm) thick. Place a sheet of plastic wrap over the butterflied flank steak and lightly pound with a meat mallet until the flank is a uniform thickness. Set aside.

• Pour Sleeman Fine Porter into a glass dish large enough to hold the open flank steak. Add garlic, Dijon mustard, herbs and pepper. Stir. Add flank steak, turning to coat. Cover and refrigerate for 24 hours to marinate.

LONDON BROIL FILLING: On the next day, combine ground beef, garlic, onion, olives, herbs, mustard, Bone Dust BBQ Seasoning, salt, Worcestershire sauce and hot sauce in a mixing bowl. Mix thoroughly; set aside.

• Remove flank steak from Porter marinade; discard leftover marinade. Pat flank steak dry with paper towel and lay flat on a cutting board.

• Form the ground-meat mixture into a roll the same length as the flank steak. Place the ground-meat roll on the bottom ⅓ of the flank steak, running the full length of the flank. It should look like a log of ground meat about 2–3 inches (5–8 cm) in diameter.

• Working from the bottom end, roll the flank steak around the ground-meat mixture, pressing firmly to preserve the log shape. Using butcher's twine, tie the London broil snugly, but not too tightly, closed every 2 inches (5 cm). Cover, refrigerate and rest for 1 hour.

• Preheat grill to medium-high heat. Remove meat from refrigerator and slice between strings to form four 2-inch (5 cm) thick, stuffed flank steak medallions. Evenly space steaks on wine-soaked plank and plank grill for 30 to 35 minutes, basting liberally with barbecue sauce during the final 10 to 15 minutes of cooking time, until the ground meat is fully cooked but still juicy. Remove from grill; cut away strings and serve.

• Serve with chilled Sleeman Fine Porter.

SERVES 4

PLANK-ROASTED MARROWBONES

1	regular hickory plank, soaked in water	1
	Aluminum foil	
2 lb	medium beef or large veal marrowbones (approximately 6 to 8 bones each cut about 2–3 inches (5–8 cm) long)	1 kg
3 Tbsp	coarsely ground sea salt or fleur de sel	45 mL
3 Tbsp	coarsely ground fresh black pepper	45 mL
1	baguette, sliced or torn into chunks	1

• Preheat grill to medium-high heat. Pat bones dry with paper towel.

• In a bowl, combine sea salt and pepper. Season both ends of the bones liberally with sea salt mixture.

• Cut a 4-inch (10 cm) square of aluminum foil for each bone. Place largest end of each bone down on a square of aluminum foil; crimp the foil around the base of the bone to make a little foil tray to catch any drippings. Repeat with remaining bones.

• Evenly space bones on plank. Place plank on grill and close lid. Plank grill the seasoned marrowbones for 20 to 30 minutes, until the bones are golden brown and about 25 percent of the marrow has melted and become liquid.

• Remove bones from grill. Transfer to a serving platter. Serve with a small spoon or knife to scoop out the hot marrow and spread onto the bread.

SERVES 4

NOTE: If you overcook these bones, you will end up with nothing to eat—because all the marrow will melt away. You want to melt only about 25 percent of the fat so that you get lots of hot, rich marrow to spread on the fresh bread.

PLANKED BEEF TENDERLOIN
WITH SMOKY MASHED POTATOES

2	regular cedar planks, soaked in water	2

SMOKY MASHED POTATOES:

8	large Yukon Gold potatoes, peeled and quartered	8
½ cup	table cream	125 mL
2 Tbsp	butter, softened	30 mL
¼ cup	chopped fresh parsley and/or fresh chives	60 mL
	Salt and freshly ground black pepper	
4	beef tenderloin fillets, 8 oz (250 g) each	4
¼ cup	Sweet Spice Rub (p. 48)	60 mL
1 cup	cheese curds, white or yellow	250 mL

David Coulson's mashed-potatoes-wrapped-beef-tenderloin has got to be one of my all-time favorite plank recipes. Try it.

SMOKY MASHED POTATOES: Place potatoes in a large pot of cold, salted water; bring to a boil. Cook for 20 minutes, until tender. Drain well and set aside for 10 to 15 minutes, until moisture has evaporated from the surface of the potatoes. Meanwhile, combine cream and butter in a saucepan and warm slightly. Add warm butter mixture to potatoes and mash, leaving some small lumps. Add chopped parsley or chives and season with salt and pepper to taste. Cool potatoes to room temperature, cover and refrigerate overnight.

• Preheat grill to high heat. Season steaks with Sweet Spice Rub, pressing the spices gently into the flesh to adhere. Sear steaks for 2 to 3 minutes on one side. Reduce heat to medium.

• Place the steaks, seared side up, evenly spaced on planks. Mold an equal amount of the mashed potatoes around each steak into a ring approximately 2-inches (5 cm) thick, leaving the top of the steaks exposed. Place planks on grill and close lid. Plank roast steak and potatoes for 20 minutes for medium-rare. The potatoes should be golden brown and crisp on the outside.

• Open grill lid and top steaks with cheese curds. Close lid and allow cheese to melt.

• Carefully remove the smoking plank from the grill and allow steaks to rest for 5 minutes before serving.

SERVES 4

RED WINE–PLANKED PEPPERCORN NEW YORK STRIP STEAKS

1	regular cedar plank, soaked in red wine/water mixture	1	
1	head plank-roasted garlic (see Cedar Plank–Roasted Garlic Soup p. 51)	1	
2	green onions, chopped	2	
¾ cup	seedless red grapes, halved	175 mL	
¼ cup	crumbled Gorgonzola cheese	60 mL	
1 Tbsp	fresh Italian parsley, chopped	15 mL	
	Salt and freshly ground pepper		
2	New York strip steaks, 12 oz (375 g) each	2	
¼ cup	multicolored peppercorns, coarsely crushed	60 mL	
	Coarse salt		
½ cup	Lindemans Bin 50 Shiraz	125 mL	

The ultimate meat-and-potatoes dish is a thick steak grilled quickly on one side and then wrapped in mashed potatoes before transferring it to a plank to finish cooking. The potatoes will keep the steak insulated so it never dries out.

• Remove the cloves of roasted garlic from the head and discard the peels. Toss the garlic, green onion, grapes, cheese and parsley together. Season with salt and pepper to taste; set aside.

• Rub the steaks with peppercorns and coarse salt. Place the steaks into a nonreactive dish and pour the red wine over. Marinate for 1 hour.

• Preheat grill to medium-high heat. Remove steaks from marinade and discard liquid. Place steaks onto grill and sear one side for 1 to 2 minutes. Turn steaks and sear opposite side for an additional 1 to 2 minutes. Remove steaks from grill and place onto plank.

• Place plank on grill and close lid. Plank grill the steaks for 10 minutes. Top steaks with roasted garlic mixture. Plank grill for 5 more minutes for medium-rare doneness. Remove plank from grill and allow steaks to rest for 2 to 3 minutes before slicing. Carve steaks into thick slices and serve immediately, spooning any garlic mixture that falls off back over the meat.

• Serve with Lindemans Bin 50 Shiraz.

SERVES 2 TO 4

PLANKED BEEF SIRLOIN STEAK
SMOTHERED IN ONIONS

1	regular oak, maple or hickory plank, soaked in water	1
4	beef sirloin steak medallions, about 6 oz (175 g) each and 1½-inches (4 cm) thick	4
2 Tbsp	Sweet Spice Rub (p. 48)	30 mL
4	thick strips Smoky Plank Bacon (p. 207) or store-bought-thick, sliced bacon	4
4	cloves garlic, minced	4
2	large sweet onions, thinly sliced	2
½ cup	Jack Daniel's Whiskey	125 mL
2 Tbsp	olive oil	30 mL
1 Tbsp	chopped fresh parsley	15 mL
	Cedar-Planked White Cheddar Mashed Potatoes (p. 228)	

• Rub each steak with 1 tsp (5 mL) of Sweet Spice Rub, pressing the seasoning into the meat so that it adheres. Tightly wrap a strip of bacon around each steak and secure with a toothpick; set aside.

• In a bowl, combine the remaining Sweet Spice Rub, garlic, sweet onions, ¼ cup (60 mL) of whiskey, olive oil and parsley. Mix well and allow onions to rest for 30 minutes.

• Preheat grill to high heat. Sear steaks only on one side for 1 to 2 minutes and remove from grill. Place steaks, seared side up, evenly spaced on plank. Cover steaks with marinated onions.

• Reduce grill heat to medium-high heat. Place plank on grill and close lid. Plank grill for 15 to 20 minutes for medium-rare, checking periodically to see that the plank is not on fire.

• When the steaks are done to your desired doneness, reduce grill flame to low. Carefully drizzle the remaining Jack Daniel's Whiskey over the onion-smothered steaks. Be careful! If the grill is set too high, the liquor will ignite and flambé. (**NOTE:** If you wish it to flambé, keep grill lid open and stand back. It looks nice and burns the alcohol off, but this step is not necessary.)

• Remove steaks from grill. Allow to rest for 5 minutes. Serve steaks with lots of smothered onions and Cedar-Planked White Cheddar Mashed Potatoes.

SERVES 4

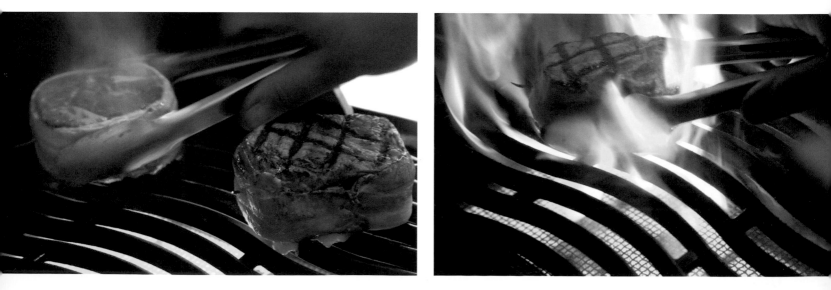

SURF AND TURF ROLL UPS

1	regular cedar, maple or oak plank, soaked in water for a minimum of 1 hour	1
4 x 5 oz	New York Strip loin steaks	4 x 150 g
2 Tbsp	olive oil	30 mL
½ cup + 1 oz	Gentleman Jack Whiskey	125 ml + 30 mL
4 cloves	garlic, minced	4
1 Tbsp	chopped fresh rosemary	15 ml
12	asparagus spears.	12
2 Tbsp	Sweet Spice Rub (p. 45)	30 ml
1 cup	cooked lobster meat (if using frozen lobster meat, be sure to squeeze excess moisture from the meat)	250 g
2 Tbsp	oyster sauce	45 ml
12	toothpicks	12
3 Tbsp	butter	45 ml
½ cup	panko Japanese bread crumbs	125 g
4 cloves	plank-smoked roasted garlic or roasted garlic, minced	4

- Trim all of the external fat from the stiploin steaks.

- Place steaks, one at a time between two sheets of plastic wrap and using a meat mallet pound the steaks out to a thickness of ¼ inch. Nice and thin.

- In a bowl combine olive oil, Gentleman Jack, garlic and rosemary. Dip flattened steaks into Gentleman Jack marinade and place in a glass dish and allow to marinate for 1 hour.

- Blanch the asparagus spears in boiling salted water for 2 minutes, remove and cool under cold running water. Pat dry with paper towel. Trim the asparagus spears to a length of 4–5 inches. Discard cut stems of asparagus. Set aside.

- Remove steaks from Gentleman Jack marinade and season steaks on both sides with seafood planking spice. Lay steaks flat on a clean work surface.

- Take a quarter cup of lobster meat and gently squeeze it so that it sticks a little together. Place on the bottom end of the steak. Place three spears of asparagus on top of the lobster with the flower end of the asparagus slightly sticking over the edge of the steak.

- Starting at the bottom of the steak, roll up with steak around the lobster and asparagus into a tight cigar-shaped roll. Secure with a toothpick to hold the roll together. Repeat with remaining steaks, lobster and asparagus.

- Place surf and turf rollups evenly spaced onto soaked plank and set aside.

- Preheat grill to medium high, approximately 450°–550°F (230°–290°C).

- In a bowl, combine oyster sauce and Gentleman Jack. Set aside.

- In a small pot over medium-low heat melt the butter. Add the panko bread crumbs and purée of smoke roasted garlic and stir until all the bread crumbs are moist and the mixture forms a paste. Set aside.

- Place planked Surf and Turf Steak Rollups onto grill and baste with oyster sauce/Gentleman Jack mixture. Close lid and cook for 15–18 minutes.

- Halfway through the cooking process spread the butter and bread crumb mixture evenly over top of the rollups to form a crust. Close lid and continue cooking. (I like to cook these to medium doneness.)

- Remove from grill and allow to rest for 3–5 minutes. Slice each surf and turf rollup into 6 rounds and serve drizzled with extra oyster sauce and Gentleman Jack mixture.

SERVES 4

MOUSSAKA

1	Plank Roasting Pan (p. 36), soaked in water	1
	Nonstick cooking spray	
2	large eggplants	2
¼ cup	kosher salt	60 mL
1⅓ cups	olive oil	325 mL
2 lb	ground lamb	1 kg
3 Tbsp	Bone Dust BBQ Seasoning (p. 46)	45 mL
10	cloves garlic, minced	10
1	large sweet onion, finely diced	1
1 cup	Spicy Tomato Sauce (p. 81) or other tomato sauce	250 mL
2 Tbsp	chopped fresh oregano	30 mL
	Salt and pepper	
4 cups	white sauce (p. 255), fully cooled	1 L
1 cup	grated feta cheese	250 mL

TIP: Salting the eggplant removes a lot of the excess moisture, as well as some of the bitterness.

• Rinse eggplants under cold, running water; pat dry and slice into ½-inch (1 cm) thick rounds. Sprinkle a cookie sheet liberally with some kosher salt. Place an even layer of sliced eggplant onto the salted cookie sheet. Sprinkle tops of eggplant slices with additional salt. Allow salted eggplant to stand for 30 minutes. Rinse well under cold, running water and pat dry with paper towel.

• Preheat grill to medium-high. Brush the eggplant slices with about 1 cup (250 mL) olive oil and grill for 4 to 5 minutes per side until the eggplant is lightly charred and tender. Remove from grill and cool.

• In a bowl, combine ground lamb and Bone Dust BBQ Seasoning. Heat ¼ cup (60 mL) of olive oil in a large frying pan set over high heat. Sauté seasoned ground lamb, stirring frequently until fully cooked. Transfer to a colander and drain. You may have to fry the ground lamb in batches so that you retain as much of the natural juices in the lamb as possible; set aside.

• In the same frying pan, heat 2 Tbsp (30 mL) of olive oil and sauté the garlic and onions for 2 to 3 minutes, stirring occasionally, until tender.

• In a large bowl, combine sautéed ground lamb, onion mixture, Spicy Tomato Sauce and oregano. Season with salt and pepper to taste. Set aside to cool. **NOTE:** This meat mixture should be thick and spoonable, not runny and pourable.

• Spray the bottom of the Plank Roasting Pan with nonstick cooking spray. Divide the sliced eggplant into three equal amounts. Arrange one portion in an even layer over the bottom of the box. Spread half of the meat mixture evenly across the eggplant.

• Spoon one-third of the white sauce evenly over the ground lamb layer.

• Sprinkle one-third of the grated feta cheese over top of the white sauce (page 255). Repeat layers with remaining ingredients. Wrap in plastic and refrigerate for 1 hour to allow all to set.

• Preheat grill to medium heat. Place plank moussaka on grill and plank bake for 45 to 60 minutes, until heated through and fully cooked. The eggplant should be tender and the casserole should be bubbling. Remove from grill and rest for 10 to 15 minutes.

• Slice into big squares to serve.

SERVES 8

BED OF HOT COALS STEAKS

1	pair of very long tongs	1
2	New York strip loin steaks, about 1 lb (500 g) each and 2-inches (5 cm) thick	2
	Salt and freshly ground black pepper	

I have been known to be a little crazy when it comes to grilling. I don't think I need to be institutionalized, but I just feel there are no boundaries when it comes to my passion for BBQ. So my friends weren't that surprised when I put our steaks directly into the hot coals of my bonfire pit. I covered the steaks with more charcoal and let the steaks cook in a bed of hot coals. It seems nuts and you might think that the ash gets all over the steak, but trust me, if your fire is just right, your steaks will be perfectly cooked!

• Prepare the fire to the point where there are plenty of hot, glowing coals. (**NOTE:** If you are working with a hardwood bonfire, it will take some time to get the fire down to hot coals. Hickory is a great wood with incredible flavor for this recipe. If using a charcoal fire in a grill, heat the coals to white hot, meaning the charcoal is no longer black and is covered with a thin layer of light-colored ash.)

• Season steaks with enough salt and pepper to coat evenly.

• Using a long pair of tongs and BBQ or welder's gloves, place the steaks directly into the hot coals. Cover steaks with additional hot charcoal or wood coals but none of the ash from the bottom of the fire which can create unpleasant flavors and coat the steak with powdery, white ash. Now take a long cool drink and wait.

• The following are the cooking times for various degrees of doneness:

  10 minutes for rare

  15 minutes for medium-rare

  18 minutes for medium

  20 minutes for medium-well

  20+ for well done

• Carefully brush the hot coals from the steak using the tongs and remove steaks from coals. Brush off any ash. Allow steaks to rest for 5 minutes. Slice each steak into ½-inch (1 cm) thick slices and serve immediately.

SERVES 2 TO 4

ROLL IN THE HAY WRAPPED STEAKS

4	big handfuls of clean hay	4
3 to 4	bottles Sleeman Honey Brown Lager	3 to 4
4	cloves garlic, minced	4
¼ cup	chopped fresh herbs, such as parsley, sage and thyme	60 mL
¼ cup	honey	60 mL
2 Tbsp	Sweet Spice Rub (p. 48)	30 mL
2 Tbsp	balsamic vinegar	30 mL
1 Tbsp	soy sauce	15 mL
4	New York Strip steaks, 12 oz (375 g) each	4

Remember that it is important to grill this recipe in an open area and not on a balcony or under an awning.

• In a large bucket or bin, soak the hay in the beer for at least 30 minutes.

• In a bowl, mix together the garlic, herbs, honey, Sweet Spice Rub, vinegar and soy sauce. Rub the garlic herb mixture into the steaks, pressing the seasoning firmly into the meat to adhere.

• Remove a handful of hay from the beer and shake off excess liquid. Lay the hay flat on a work surface; spread evenly to the approximate length of a steak. Place one steak at the bottom end of the hay. Carefully roll the steak in the hay until well covered. Repeat this process for the remaining steaks. Approximately half of the hay should remain unused.

• Preheat grill to high heat. Place hay-wrapped steaks on grill, top with remaining hay and close lid. Allow the steaks to smoke in the hay for 12 to 15 minutes. **NOTE:** There will be a lot of smoke but do not open the grill lid. Leave it to smoke.

• Carefully open grill lid and stand back. When the lid opens, the hay will catch fire and burn off quickly. Allow as much of the hay to burn off as possible. As the flames die down, use a long pair of grill tongs, pick up each steak and knock off any excess hay.

• At this point steaks should be a nice medium-rare. For well done, continue to grill the steaks. Remove steaks from grill and rest for 5 minutes. Drizzle with extra beer and serve.

SERVES 4

SMOKIN' BEER-PLANKED BACK RIBS WITH NUTS

1	regular maple plank, soaked in beer/water mixture or water	1
2	racks pork back ribs, each rack approx. 1½ lbs (750 g)	2
¼ cup	Bone Dust BBQ Seasoning (p. 46)	60 mL
4	cloves garlic, minced	4
4	chili peppers, chopped	4
1	medium onion, finely diced	1
2	limes, thinly sliced	2
1 cup	Fire-Roasted Hickory-Planked BBQ Sauce (p. 227) (approx.)	250 mL
¼ cup	Sleeman Original Dark Ale	60 mL
¼ cup	crushed peanuts	60 mL
¼ cup	brown sugar	60 mL

• Using a sharp knife, score the membrane on the backside of the ribs in a diamond pattern. Rub with Bone Dust BBQ Seasoning, pressing the seasoning into the meat.

• Preheat oven to 325°F (160°C). Place the plank into a large roasting pan. Pour in beer/water mixture until the plank floats. Scatter the garlic, chili peppers and onion evenly over the surface of the plank. Lay the ribs, meat side down, on top of the plank. Lay 3 to 4 slices of lime on the top of each rack.

• Cover with lid or aluminum foil. Place pan in the oven and braise plank ribs for 2 to 2½ hours, until tender and meat pulls easily from bones.

• Meanwhile, combine Fire-Roasted Hickory-Planked BBQ Sauce and beer, stir and set aside.

• Remove ribs from oven and cool slightly. Transfer ribs to a rimmed baking sheet and discard cooking liquid and garlic, chili peppers and onion; reserve plank. Cut the ribs into 3-bone sections. Brush rib sections all over with some of the barbecue sauce and stack on reserved plank.

• Preheat grill to medium heat. Plank grill ribs for 15 to 20 minutes, basting occasionally with any remaining Fire-Roasted Hickory-Planked BBQ Sauce, until ribs are lightly smoky, heated through, and slightly crispy.

• Sprinkle with crushed peanuts and brown sugar and close grill lid. Allow to cook for another 5 minutes, until peanuts and brown sugar are hot and sticky. Remove from grill.

Serve with extra sauce.

SERVES 4

HICKORY PLANK–SMOKED ST. LOUIS RIBS

1	thick hickory plank, 12-inch (30 cm) x 18-inches (45 cm) x 1½-inches (4 cm) thick, soaked in water for a minimum of 2 hours	1
1	rib rack barbecue accessory	1
3	racks St. Louis cut pork spareribs, about 1½–2 lbs (750 g–1 kg) each	3
4	bottles Sleeman Original Cream Ale	4
1½ cups	Jack Daniel's Whiskey	375 mL
6 Tbsp	Bone Dust BBQ Seasoning (p. 46)	90 mL
2 cups	Ted Reader's World Famous BBQ Crazy Canuck Sticky Chicken and Rib Sauce or your favorite gourmet-style BBQ sauce (approx.)	500 mL
½ cup	maple syrup	125 mL

If all you have is a gas grill yet you want to have smoked ribs, this is the recipe you need. It gives you real southern BBQ ribs without all the trouble of having a smoker.

• Lay ribs in single layer in a large container and pour over 3 bottles of beer and 1 cup (250 mL) of the Jack Daniel's, turning to coat evenly. Cover and refrigerate for 24 hours, allowing the alcohol mixture to marinate the ribs. Remove ribs from marinade, discarding the liquid.

• Pat ribs dry with paper towel. Rub ribs liberally with Bone Dust BBQ Seasoning, pressing the seasoning into the meat so that it adheres; set aside.

• In a bowl, combine barbecue sauce, maple syrup and remaining Jack Daniel's; set aside.

• Preheat grill to low heat. It's important to keep the grill temperature low; the temperature should stay between 180°F (82°C) and 225°F (107°C).

• Place plank on grill; top with rib rack and place the seasoned ribs in the rib rack. Loosely cover or tent with a piece of aluminum foil. Close lid and allow the ribs to plank smoke for 3 hours, basting occasionally with remaining beer. Plank smoke for 1 hour longer, basting the ribs with the reserved barbecue sauce mixture. The ribs are done once the bone separates from the meat when wiggled. Remove ribs from grill and serve with extra BBQ sauce and cold beer.

SERVES 6 TO 8

TIP: St. Louis cut pork spareribs are prepared by removing the cartilage and the rib tips from the rack to make a clean rectangular shape.

PLANK ROAST RACK OF PORK BASTED
WITH APPLE HONEY BUTTER

1	thick apple or hickory plank, soaked in water or apple cider/water mixture	1
1	Cajun-style injector syringe	1
1	frenched rack of pork, approximately 6–7 bones, 4–5 lbs (2–2.5 kg)	1
2 cups	apple cider	500 mL
½ cup	Jack Daniel's Whiskey	125 mL
¼ cup	Sweet Spice Rub (p. 48)	60 mL

APPLE-HONEY BUTTER:

½ cup	honey	125 mL
¼ cup	apple butter	60 mL
2 Tbsp	Dijon mustard	30 mL
2 Tbsp	butter	30 mL
1 oz.	Jack Daniel's Whiskey	30 mL

• Place rack of pork into a large pan, about 4–5-inches (10–12 cm) deep. Add apple cider and Jack Daniel's. Using a Cajun injector,* suck up a syringe full of the apple cider mixture. Inject it into a number of different points in the pork. Repeat twice more in different spots. Cover and refrigerate for 24 hours, turning occasionally.

• Place a drip pan, half filled with water, under one side of the grate. Preheat grill to medium-high.

• Place plank on grill and close grill lid. Heat plank for a few minutes until it begins to crackle and smoke.

• Remove pork from apple cider marinade, discarding leftover marinade in the pan. Dry outside of the rack of pork with paper towel. Evenly coat pork with Sweet Spice Rub. Set aside. Place the pork on the plank and let it sear cook for 15 minutes.

APPLE-HONEY BUTTER: Meanwhile, in a small pot set over medium heat, stir together honey, apple butter, mustard, butter and Jack Daniel's; keep warm.

• Reduce grill heat to 325°F (160°) and continue cooking for 1 hour. Baste the pork with the honey mixture; close grill lid and continue to plank roast for 10 more minutes. The internal temperature of the pork loin should be 150°F (65°C) for medium doneness.

• Remove plank from grill. Let the meat rest for 5 to 10 minutes to allow the juices to redistribute before carving. The meat should have a touch of pink to it. Slice between each bone and serve.

• Serve with Lindemans Bin 45 Cabernet Sauvignon.

SERVES 6

*NOTE: A Cajun injector is a large handheld tool that resembles a syringe. It's used to inject flavor right into meats and cheeses so that they marinate from the inside out.

CEDAR-PLANKED FRENCHED RACK OF VEAL
WITH APRICOT-BACON STUFFING

1	thick cedar plank, soaked in white wine/water mixture	1

APRICOT-BACON STUFFING:

4	slices double-smoked bacon, diced	4
3	ribs celery, diced	3
1	medium onion, diced	1
2 Tbsp	butter	30 mL
1 cup	diced dried apricots	250 mL
⅓ cup	Seafood Plank Seasoning (p. 45)	75 mL
2 Tbsp	chopped fresh parsley	30 mL
1 Tbsp	chopped fresh sage	15 mL
6 cups	small cubes, dried sourdough bread	1.5 L
3 Tbsp	Lindemans Bin 65 Chardonnay or other white wine	45 mL
½ cup	apricot jam	125 mL
¼ cup	maple syrup	60 mL
2 Tbsp	Grand Marnier liqueur	30 mL
1 Tbsp	grainy mustard	15 mL
1	frenched rack of white veal, 5–7 bones, 5 lbs (2.5 kg)	1

• Preheat grill to medium heat.

APRICOT-BACON STUFFING: In a large frying pan set over medium-high heat, sauté the bacon for 4 to 5 minutes, until slightly crisp. Add the celery, onion and butter. Continue to sauté, stirring frequently, for 2 to 3 minutes until the onions are tender. Add the apricots and sauté for 1 minute. Remove from heat and season this mixture with 1 Tbsp (15 mL) Seafood Plank Seasoning and the herbs. Add mixture to bread cubes. Toss gently and moisten with wine. Mix thoroughly; set aside.

• In a medium bowl, combine apricot jam, maple syrup, Grand Marnier and grainy mustard. Mix well to combine and cover; set aside.

• Carefully make a hole in one end of the veal rack. Use a sharp knife to cut down through the eye of the meat. The cut should be about 2-inches (5 cm) in diameter. Place the bread mixture into a piping bag with a ½-inch (1 cm) opening at the end. Squeeze the stuffing into the center of the veal, packing it into the opening made by the knife. Season the outside of the veal with the remaining Seafood Plank Seasoning, pressing seasoning into the meat.

• Place stuffed veal rack on plank. Place plank on grill and close lid. Plank grill veal for 1 hour (approximately 15 to 20 minutes per pound) or until stuffing registers minimum internal temperature of 165°F (74°C) when checked with an instant-read thermometer. During the final 15 to 20 minutes of cooking, baste liberally with reserved maple mixture. Close lid and continue to plank grill until glaze is caramelized.

• Remove from grill and allow to rest for 5 minutes before serving. Slice between each bone and serve.

SERVES 6

101 CLOVES OF GARLIC PRIME RIB
WITH RED WINE BUTTER INJECTION

1	large, thick oak plank, soaked in red wine/water mixture	1
1	Cajun style injector syringe	1
1	bone-in prime rib roast, 6–8 lbs (3–3.5 kg)	
¼ cup	Sweet Spice Rub (p. 48)	60 mL
101	cloves plank-roasted garlic, smashed (see Cedar Plank–Roasted Garlic Soup, p. 51)	101
3 Tbsp	olive oil	45 mL
3 Tbsp	honey	45 mL
3 Tbsp	Dijon mustard	45 mL
2 Tbsp	fresh rosemary, chopped	30 mL
2 Tbsp	prepared horseradish (approx.)	30 mL
1 cup	Lindemans BIN 50 Shiraz	250 mL
½ cup	melted butter	125 mL

• Preheat grill to high heat.

• Rub the prime rib with the Sweet Spice Rub, pressing firmly into the meat so that it adheres. Mix together the 101 cloves of roasted garlic, oil, honey, mustard, rosemary and prepared horseradish; set aside.

• Place plank on grill and heat for 5 minutes until it starts to crackle and smoke. Place seasoned prime rib roast directly on the plank and roast for 15 minutes at 450°F (232°C). Reduce heat until grill holds a steady 350°F (176°C) temperature. Spread the roasted garlic mixture evenly over the top of the prime rib.

• Continue to roast for 1½ to 1¾ hours (approximately 20 minutes per pound) for medium doneness, 150°F (65°C). Halfway through the cooking process, combine the red wine and melted butter. Using the Cajun injector (see p. 192 for definition), suck the wine mixture into the injector chamber and inject into the prime rib in several places.

• When the prime rib is done, remove plank from grill; loosely cover with foil and allow to rest for 15 minutes before carving. Slice prime rib thickly or thinly as suits your taste and serve with additional prepared horseradish on the side.

• Serve with Lindemans Bin 50 Shiraz.

SERVES 8

PLANKED THAI RACK OF LAMB

1	regular hickory or cedar plank, soaked in water	1
2	frenched lamb racks, 1½ lb (750 g) each	2
½ cup	soy sauce	125 mL
¼ cup	peanut or vegetable oil	60 mL
¼ cup	tamarind paste, strained	60 mL
¼ cup	rice vinegar	60 mL
¼ cup	chopped fresh cilantro	60 mL
3 Tbsp	brown sugar	45 mL
3	red chilies, minced	3
2	cloves garlic, minced	2
2	green onions, thinly sliced	2
2	limes, zested and juiced	2
½ cup	coconut milk	125 mL
2 Tbsp	Bone Dust BBQ Seasoning (p. 46)	30 mL

The flavors of cilantro, lime, coconut and chili pepper blend well with the flavors of lamb and the hickory plank. If you cannot find hickory planks, try this recipe with cherry or apple wood planks. If you like your food really spicy, add additional chili to the marinade.

• In a large bowl, whisk together soy sauce, peanut oil, tamarind paste, rice vinegar, cilantro, brown sugar, chilies, garlic, green onions, lime zest and juice. Set aside ½ cup (125 mL) of the marinade.

• Pour remaining marinade over the lamb racks, turning to coat evenly. Cover and refrigerate for a minimum of 2 hours or marinate overnight, turning occasionally.

• Preheat grill to medium-high heat. Pour coconut milk and reserved marinade into a small saucepan and bring to a simmer set over medium-high heat. Reduce heat to low and simmer until sauce thickens enough to coat the back of a spoon. Remove from heat and keep warm.

• Remove lamb racks from marinade. Season lamb with Bone Dust BBQ Seasoning and place on plank, crossing the bones from each rack to form an X above the plank. Close lid and plank grill the lamb racks for 12 to 15 minutes. Open lid and baste lamb liberally with sauce. Close lid and continue to plank grill for an additional 3 to 4 minutes for medium-rare. Remove plank from grill and allow to rest for 5 minutes.

• Slice lamb between each bone and serve with coconut-enhanced sauce for dipping.

SERVES 4

MESQUITE PLANK ROAST LEG OF LAMB
WITH CHIMICHURRI SAUCE

1	thick mesquite or oak or maple plank, soaked in water	1
1	bone-in leg of lamb, approx. 5 lbs (2.5 kg)	1
3 Tbsp	Sweet Spice Rub (p. 48)	45 mL

CHIMICHURRI SAUCE:

20	cloves garlic, minced	20
½ bunch	fresh parsley, finely chopped	½
½ bunch	fresh cilantro, finely chopped	½
½ cup	malt vinegar	125 mL
½ cup	olive oil	125 mL
¼ cup	lime juice	60 mL
¼ cup	rum	60 mL
1–2 Tbsp	Sambal olek hot chili sauce (approx.)	15–30 mL
2 tsp	smoked paprika	10 mL
2 tsp	cracked black pepper	10 mL
2 tsp	kosher salt	10 mL
2 tsp	minced ginger	10 mL

• Preheat grill to medium-high heat. Rub leg of lamb with Sweet Spice Rub, pressing the spices into the meat so that it adheres; set aside.

CHIMICHURRI SAUCE: In a canning jar, combine garlic, parsley, cilantro, vinegar, olive oil, lime juice, rum, hot sauce, smoked paprika, black pepper, salt and ginger. Close jar lid and shake until evenly combined. Set aside half for basting.

• Place plank on grill and close lid for 1 to 2 minutes until the plank starts to crackle and smoke. Place leg of lamb on plank and close lid. Roast leg of lamb for 15 minutes to sear in the juices.

• Reduce heat to medium and continue to roast lamb, basting every 10 minutes with reserved Chimichurri Sauce, until leg of lamb is cooked to medium, approximately 70 to 90 minutes, or until it registers 150°F (65°C) on an instant-read thermometer.

• Remove lamb from grill. Allow meat to rest for 10 minutes. Carve and serve with remaining Chimichurri Sauce for dipping.

SERVES 4 TO 6

PLANKED VENISON TENDERLOIN
WITH RASPBERRY GLAZING SYRUP

1	regular maple or oak plank, soaked in water	1
¼ cup	Seafood Plank Seasoning (p. 45)	60 mL
¼ cup	Dijon mustard	60 mL
¼ cup	Lindemans Bin 40 Merlot	60 mL
2 Tbsp	olive oil	30 mL
2 Tbsp	grainy mustard	30 mL
2 Tbsp	chopped fresh parsley	30 mL
2	frenched venison racks, 1¼–1½ lbs (625–750 g) each	2
1 cup	coarsely chopped pistachio nuts	250 mL
	Raspberry Glazing Syrup, divided (recipe follows)	

RASPBERRY GLAZING SYRUP:

2 Tbsp	olive oil	30 mL
3	cloves garlic, minced	3
3	shallots, diced	3
½ cup	balsamic vinegar	125 mL
1½ cups	fresh or frozen raspberries	375 mL
2	sprigs thyme	2
1 cup	maple syrup	250 mL
1 tsp	black pepper, cracked	5 mL
	Salt	

MAKES APPROXIMATELY 1 CUP (250 ML)

It may seem like an odd combination but the sweet, yet tart flavor of the raspberry glaze is the perfect balance to the gamey flavor of the venison. Don't save this syrup just for planking; it's also great on French toast, pancakes and the one you love.

• In a bowl, mix together the Seafood Plank Seasoning, Dijon mustard, wine, oil, grainy mustard and parsley to form a thick paste; set aside.

• Pat racks of venison dry with paper towel. Using a sharp knife, cut each rack into three 3-inch (8 cm) thick chops, each containing 2 bones. Place venison chops in a glass baking dish and pour mustard mixture over meat; turn to coat each chop evenly. Marinate, covered, in the refrigerator for 3 to 4 hours. Preheat grill to medium-high heat. Place plank on grill; close lid and heat for 5 minutes until plank starts to crackle and smoke.

• Remove venison chops from marinade and scrape off the marinade. Stand venison chops upright on plank so that bones point up and touch to support each chop. Close lid and roast for 15 to 18 minutes for medium doneness. Baste 2 or 3 times with a little of one half of the prepared Raspberry Glazing Syrup during cooking. When venison chops are just done, glaze liberally with Raspberry Glazing Syrup and sprinkle with pistachios.

• Remove chops from the grill and rest for 5 minutes. Using a sharp knife, slice piece of meat in half to make two chops. Serve with reserved Raspberry Glazing Syrup and a glass of Lindemans Bin 40 Merlot.

SERVES 6

RASPBERRY GLAZING SYRUP: Heat the oil in a medium saucepan set over medium-high heat. Sauté the garlic and shallots for 2 to 3 minutes, until tender.

• Deglaze the saucepan with balsamic vinegar and reduce liquid by half by simmering for several minutes. Add raspberries and continue to cook for 3 minutes, stirring and slightly mashing the raspberries to extract the juice. Add thyme sprigs, maple syrup and black pepper. Bring to boil and reduce heat to medium. Let simmer for 10 to 15 minutes.

• Using a hand blender or food processor, purée the raspberry mixture until smooth. Strain out seeds and season the sauce to taste with salt and cool. Divide sauce in half.

SAUSAGE ON A STICK

1	Vertical Plank (p. 40), soaked in water for 1 hour	1
12	hardwood skewers, about 10-inches (25 cm) in length	12
12	smoked sausages, your favorite kind or jumbo hot dogs	12
½ cup	prepared mustard	125 mL
½ cup	honey	125 mL
¼ cup	Sleeman Original Dark Beer	60 mL

• Skewer each sausage through the entire length of the meat. Using a paring knife, make 10 to 12 small slashes down the length of each sausage on all sides. Insert pointed end of skewers into the plank.

• In a bowl, whisk prepared mustard, honey and beer until smooth.

• Place plank on grill and close lid. Plank smoke sausages for 20 to 25 minutes, basting every 5 minutes with mustard mixture, until heated through, well-browned and well-glazed. Remove from grill and serve immediately with any remaining mustard mixture.

SERVES 12

SMOKY PLANK BACON

1	thick maple, oak or hickory plank, soaked in water	1
3 Tbsp	kosher salt	45 mL
⅔ cup	Bone Dust BBQ Seasoning (p. 46)	150 mL
1	raw pork belly chunk, about 3 lbs (1.5 kg)	1

Are you tired of buying soggy, wet bacon? I am, so here's a recipe for making your own. Most of the recipes in this cookbook that call for bacon were tested using this bacon recipe.

• In a bowl, combine kosher salt with ½ cup (125 mL) Bone Dust BBQ Seasoning.

• Rinse the pork belly under cold, running water and pat dry with paper towel.

• Rub the pork belly with the kosher salt mixture, pressing and rubbing the seasoning firmly into the meat so that it adheres. Place into a glass dish, cover and refrigerate for 2 days allowing the meat to cure in the seasoning.

• Preheat grill to medium heat. Remove pork belly from refrigerator. Rinse under cold, running water and pat dry with paper towel. Sprinkle with remaining Bone Dust BBQ Seasoning. Center pork belly on plank.

• Place plank on grill and close lid. Plank smoke the pork belly for 3 hours, until an internal temperature of 170°F (76°C) is reached. Check occasionally to see that the plank has not caught on fire and that the pork is smoking nicely. Remove from grill and cool completely. Use a meat slicer for thin strips or a sharp knife to slice smoked pork more thickly.

MAKES ABOUT 3 LBS (1.5 KG) OF BACON

DR. BBQ'S BANANA LEAF–WRAPPED GRILLED JERK PORK TENDERLOIN

2	banana leaves	2
	butcher twine	
2	pork tenderloins, about 20 oz (600 g) each, trimmed	2
1	bottle Sleeman Original Cream Ale	1
	Jamaican Jerk Paste (recipe follows)	
2 Tbsp	butter, softened	30 mL
8	sprigs of cilantro	8
2	green onions, chopped	2
1	small red onion, thinly sliced	1
1	orange, peeled and segmented	1
1	lime, peeled and segmented	1
1	lemon, peeled and segmented	1
1	mango, peeled, thinly sliced and cut into julienne strips	1
	Salt and pepper	

JAMAICAN JERK PASTE:

6	green onions, coarsely chopped	6
4	Scotch bonnet peppers	4
¼ cup	water	60 mL
6	cloves garlic	6
1 cup	lightly packed fresh cilantro leaves	250 mL
1 cup	lightly packed fresh parsley leaves	250 mL
¼ cup	olive oil	60 mL
¼ cup	lemon juice	60 mL
2 Tbsp	ground allspice	30 mL
2 tsp	salt	10 mL
1 tsp	ground cloves	5 mL
1 tsp	ground cumin	5 mL
1 tsp	black pepper	5 mL

My buddy Ray Lampe is Dr. BBQ. He is a fanatic about barbecue and everything delicious. Thanks for the recipe, Ray!

• Place tenderloins in a glass dish or large resealable plastic bag. Whisk together beer and ½ cup (125 mL) of the Jamaican Jerk Paste until smooth. Pour over tenderloins and marinate, covered, in the refrigerator, for 24 hours.

• Preheat grill to high heat. Remove pork tenderloins from marinade, discarding leftover marinade. Rub the tenderloins with soft butter. Slather pork tenderloins with remaining jerk paste; set aside.

• In a bowl, combine cilantro, green onion, red onion, orange, lime and lemon segments, and mango. Season with salt and pepper to taste. Warm a banana leaf over the hot grill for 10 to 15 seconds per side. (This releases the chlorophyll in the leaf and makes it more pliable.)

• Set banana leaf on a flat work surface. Place a quarter of the onion mixture in the center of the banana leaf. Place one pork tenderloin over the onion mixture and then top with another quarter of the onion mixture. Roll the banana leaf into a tight bundle. Secure closed with butcher's twine; set aside. Repeat with remaining ingredients.

• Place bundles on hot grill and close lid. Grill roast for 15 to 20 minutes, turning once. Remove from grill. Rest for 5 minutes. Carefully cut the twine and unwrap the banana leaves. Slice the pork tenderloin into ½-inch (1 cm) thick rounds and top with the hot onion mixture. Serve immediately.

SERVES 4

JAMAICAN JERK PASTE: In a food processor or blender, purée the green onions, Scotch bonnet peppers and water. Add the garlic, cilantro and parsley; purée until smooth. Add the olive oil, lemon juice, allspice, salt, cloves, cumin and black pepper. Blend until fully incorporated. Store in an airtight container, in the refrigerator, for up to 2 weeks.

PORK, PORK, PORK

1	regular cedar plank, soaked in water	1

MARINADE:

2	cloves garlic, minced	2
1	bottle Sleeman Original Draught	1
½	Spanish onion, minced	½
2 Tbsp	honey mustard	30 mL
2 Tbsp	chopped Italian parsley	30 mL
	Salt and pepper	
1	pork tenderloin, about 20 oz (600 g), trimmed	1
1	10-inch (25 cm) long, spicy smoked cooked sausage	1
2–3	¼-inch (5 mm) thick slices Smoky Plank Bacon (p. 207)	2–3
4	cloves garlic, chopped	4
1	large onion, sliced	1
	Mustard	

MARINADE: In a large bowl, whisk together garlic, beer, onion, honey mustard and parsley. Season with salt and pepper to taste; set aside.

• Lay pork tenderloin onto a flat surface. Using a sharp, thin knife, cut an incision lengthwise into the center of the pork tenderloin. To complete the incision, turn tenderloin around and insert knife into the opposite end, forming a tunnel the same diameter as the smoked sausage. Carefully push sausage into the cavity made in the pork tenderloin.

• Lay stuffed pork tenderloin in a glass dish; pour over reserved marinade. Cover and refrigerate for 2 hours or overnight, turning occasionally. Remove pork tenderloin from the marinade, discarding leftover marinade. Wrap pork tenderloin in bacon and secure with toothpick.

• Preheat grill to medium-high heat. Place soaked plank on a flat work surface. Scatter garlic and onions over the plank. Place pork tenderloin on the plank. Place the plank on grill and close lid. Plank smoke for 40 to 45 minutes, until pork tenderloin is just cooked to medium doneness and the smoked sausage is hot and the bacon wrap is crisp. Remove from grill. Slice and serve with your favorite mustard for dipping.

SERVES 4 TO 8

SANDWICHES

HICKORY-PLANKED SIRLOIN BURGERS
WITH BLUE CHEESE

1	regular hickory plank, soaked in beer/water mixture	1
¾ cup	dark full-bodied beer	175 mL
2 lb	ground beef sirloin	1 kg
1	small onion, finely diced	1
2 Tbsp	mashed plank-roasted garlic (see Cedar Plank–Roasted Garlic Soup, p. 51)	30 mL
2 Tbsp	Worcestershire sauce	30 mL
2 Tbsp	chopped fresh parsley	30 mL
1 Tbsp	Dijon mustard	15 mL
1 Tbsp	Bone Dust BBQ Seasoning (p. 46)	15 mL
¼ cup	olive oil	60 mL
4 cups	quartered button mushrooms	1 L
1	large Spanish onion, sliced	1
	Kosher salt and freshly ground black pepper	
1 cup	crumbled blue cheese	250 mL
4	multigrain hamburger buns or rolls	4
1	bunch arugula, washed	1
1	large ripe tomato, sliced	1

These are absolutely delicious. Period.

• Use half the beer to soak the plank. Reserve remaining beer for basting burgers.

• In a large bowl, combine ground sirloin, onion, Plank-Roasted Garlic, Worcestershire sauce, parsley, Dijon mustard and Bone Dust BBQ Seasoning. Mix well to incorporate. Form into 8 hamburgers; each burger should be about 1-inch (2.5 cm) thick and 4-inches (10 cm) in diameter. Transfer to a cookie sheet; cover and refrigerate for 1 hour to allow meat to rest before planking.

• Preheat grill to medium-high heat. Evenly space burgers on plank; place plank on grill and close lid. Plank grill burgers for 15 to 20 minutes; brush occasionally with remaining beer. Burgers are fully cooked when an instant-read thermometer inserted through the side of the burger into the center registers 160°F (71°C).

• Meanwhile, heat oil in a large frying pan until it just starts to smoke. Add mushrooms and sauté for 3 to 5 minutes, stirring occasionally, until mushrooms are lightly colored. Add onion to pan and continue to sauté, stirring occasionally, for another 3 to 5 minutes until onion is tender. Season with salt and pepper to taste. Remove from heat and cool slightly.

• Add crumbled blue cheese to mushroom mixture and gently toss. Just before the burgers are finished cooking, spoon an equal amount of the mushroom mixture over each burger. Close grill lid and continue to cook burgers for another 2 to 3 minutes until the cheese starts to melt.

• Slice burger buns in half and lightly toast buns on the grill. Serve each burger on a half bun topped with fresh arugula and sliced tomatoes.

SERVES 8

BACON AND EGG BREAKFAST BURGERS

2	regular cedar planks, soaked in water	2
1½ lb	ground pork, icy cold from the refrigerator	750 g
1	small onion, finely diced	1
¼ cup	Japanese panko bread crumbs	60 mL
3 Tbsp	Bone Dust BBQ Seasoning (p. 46)	45 mL
2 Tbsp	grated Parmesan cheese	30 mL
2 Tbsp	honey mustard	30 mL
4	slices thick-sliced bacon	4
4	small eggs	4
	Toasted English muffins	

I made this one morning as a last-minute recipe for the *City TV Morning Show* host, Jennifer Valentine.

• In a bowl, combine ground pork, onion, bread crumbs, Bone Dust BBQ Seasoning, Parmesan cheese and honey mustard. Gently blend until ingredients are well mixed. Form into four 6-oz (175 g) baseball-shaped burgers.

• Gently flatten the burgers slightly, pushing down on the center of each burger to form a well approximately 1-inch (2.5 cm) deep, allowing the egg to sit and cook evenly and not run off the burger.

• Wrap a slice of bacon around the outside of each burger and secure with a toothpick. Cover and refrigerate for 1 hour, to allow the meat to rest.

• Preheat grill to medium-high heat. Evenly space three burgers on each plank.

• Place planks on grill and close lid. Plank bake burgers for 6 to 8 minutes to allow the outside of the meat to slightly cook.

• Crack each egg into a small glass dish and pour each egg into the well of each burger. Close lid and continue to cook for 15 to 20 minutes, until an instant-read thermometer inserted through the side of the burger into the center of the meat registers 160°F (71°C), the bacon is a little crisp and the egg is cooked but the yolk is still a little runny. Remove from grill and serve on toasted English muffins.

SERVES 4

BEERLICIOUS BURGERS

2	regular maple planks, soaked in water	2
2 lb	regular ground beef, icy cold from the refrigerator	1 kg
½ cup	Sleeman Original Draught	125 mL
⅓ cup	Bone Dust BBQ Seasoning (p. 46)	75 mL
½ cup	Ted Reader's World Famous BBQ Beerlicious BBQ Sauce or your favorite smoky BBQ sauce	125 mL
6	slices American processed cheese Burger fixin's	6

My Beerlicious BBQ Sauce inspired these burgers. They truly are a mouthful and not for the timid. They are big, juicy and more than a little messy! Open wide or get a knife and fork. Truly a burger meant for a hinged jaw.

• Place the ground beef in a large bowl. Drizzle ¼ cup (60 mL) of the beer over the ground beef. Sprinkle the Bone Dust BBQ Seasoning evenly over the meat. Mix gently but thoroughly.

• Form meat mixture into 6 large, baseball-shaped burgers. **NOTE:** Do not flatten the burgers; leave them shaped like baseballs. This will help keep the burgers moist and juicy. Place burgers on a tray or plate; cover and refrigerate for 1 hour, allowing the meat to rest.

• In a bowl, combine the remaining beer with the Ted Reader's World Famous BBQ Beerlicious BBQ Sauce; set aside.

• Preheat grill to medium-high heat. Evenly space 3 burgers on each plank.

• Place planks on grill and close lid. Plank grill for 25 to 30 minutes, basting with reserved beer barbecue sauce during the last 15 minutes of planking, until an instant-read thermometer inserted through the side of the burger into the center of the meat registers 160°F (71°C).

• Top each burger with a slice of processed cheese, turn grill off and close lid allowing the cheese to melt over the meat. Remove burgers from grill and serve with a knife and fork or serve on buns with traditional burger condiments.

SERVES 6

TIP: If you serve these burgers on buns, you may need to squish them a little to get them into your mouth. I like mine on soft buns with thinly sliced red onions, crisp lettuce and a dollop of mayo.

PERFECT CHICKEN BURGERS

1	24-inch (60 cm) regular cedar plank, soaked in water	1
4	cloves garlic, minced	4
1	medium sweet onion, diced	1
1	large egg	1
2 lb	ground chicken, icy cold from the refrigerator	1 kg
1 lb	boneless, skinless chicken breasts, thinly sliced into strips	500 g
¾ cup	crispy fried onion pieces (available in Asian grocery stores)	175 mL
½ cup	Japanese panko bread crumbs	125 mL
¼ cup	grated Parmesan cheese	60 mL
1 Tbsp	Bone Dust BBQ Seasoning (p. 46)	15 mL
1 Tbsp	chopped fresh parsley	15 mL
1 Tbsp	olive oil	15 mL
8	balls bocconcini (1-in. round) cheese, frozen	8
½ cup	Lindemans Bin 65 Chardonnay	125 mL
½ cup	melted butter	125 mL
8	grape or cherry tomatoes	8

I find that most chicken burgers never have great texture. My recipe requires you to add thin strips of fresh chicken breast meat. This will provide the burger with a nice firm bite.

• In a large bowl, combine garlic, onion, egg, ground chicken, sliced chicken breast, crispy fried onion pieces, bread crumbs, Parmesan cheese, Bone Dust BBQ Seasoning, parsley and olive oil. Mix well.

• Form chicken mixture into 8 equal baseball-shaped burgers. Push a hole into the center of each burger to form a well. Place a frozen bocconcini into the center of each burger and fold the meat around to seal cheese in the center. (**NOTE:** Putting the cheese in the freezer keeps it from melting too quickly when grilling burgers.) Cover and place burgers in refrigerator for 1 hour.

• In a bowl, combine white wine and melted butter.

• Preheat grill to medium-high. Place burgers evenly spaced onto plank. Place plank on grill and close lid. Plank bake for 30 to 40 minutes, until chicken burgers are fully cooked, moist and juicy, basting with white wine butter sauce.

• Just before burgers are cooked, grill 8 grape or cherry tomatoes until lightly charred and tender. Place one charred tomato on top of each planked chicken burger. Remove from grill and serve immediately on your favorite kind of bun with burger condiments.

SERVES 8

CEDAR-PLANKED SALMON BURGER SLIDERS
WITH CUCUMBER RADISH SLAW AND DILL HAVARTI

1	regular cedar plank, soaked in white wine/ water mixture	1
½	bottle (750 mL) Lindemans Bin 65 Chardonnay	½
4 cups	cold water	1 L
1.5 lb	boneless, skinless fresh salmon fillets	750 g
2	green onions, finely chopped	2
1	egg white	1
½ cup	Japanese panko bread crumbs	125 mL
½ cup	finely diced red onion	125 mL
2 Tbsp	Seafood Plank Seasoning (p. 45)	30 mL
1 Tbsp	chopped fresh dill	15 mL
1 tsp	fresh lemon juice	5 mL
8	slices dill-flavored Havarti cheese	8
8	Planked Biscuits (p. 259), halved	8

CUCUMBER RADISH SLAW:

8	red radishes, thinly sliced and cut into matchstick-sized strips	8
1	small red onion, thinly sliced into matchstick-sized strips	1
½	seedless cucumber, cut in half lengthwise and sliced into matchstick-sized strips	½
2 Tbsp	olive oil	30 mL
2 Tbsp	chopped fresh dill	30 mL
1 Tbsp	fresh lemon juice	15 mL
	Salt and freshly ground black pepper to taste	
	splash Pinot Grigio	

TARTAR SAUCE:

½ cup	mayonnaise	125 mL
1	green onion, minced	1
1	kosher-style dill pickle, minced	1
1 tsp	chopped fresh dill	5 mL
½ tsp	lemon juice	2 mL
	Salt and freshly ground black pepper	

• Combine the wine with the water and soak plank for a minimum of 1 hour. Meanwhile, using a sharp knife, finely dice the salmon into ¼-inch (5 mm) pieces. In a bowl, mix the diced salmon, green onion, egg white, bread crumbs, red onion, Seafood Plank Seasoning, dill and lemon juice. The mixture should be a little moist and sticky, but not too dry.

• Using an ice cream scoop, form mixture into 8 miniburgers. Evenly space patties on plank. Cover with plastic wrap and refrigerate for 1 to 2 hours.

CUCUMBER RADISH SLAW: In another bowl, combine the radish, red onion, cucumber, olive oil, dill and lemon juice. Add a splash of Pinot Grigio and season to taste with salt and freshly ground black pepper. Cover and refrigerate until needed.

TARTAR SAUCE: In a third bowl, combine the mayonnaise, green onion, dill pickle, dill and lemon juice. Season with salt and pepper to taste. Cover and refrigerate until needed.

• Preheat grill to medium-high heat. Plank grill salmon burgers for 15 to 18 minutes until just about cooked through; check grill once or twice during cooking to ensure that the planks have not caught fire.

• During the last few minutes of cooking time, top each salmon burger with a slice of Havarti cheese, close lid and allow the cheese to melt.

• Open grill and carefully remove the hot planks. Using a spatula, remove salmon burgers from plank and place one planked salmon slider burger onto one Planked Biscuit. Top with reserved Cucumber Radish Slaw and Tartar Sauce.

SERVES 4–8

TIP: Serve sliders with chilled Lindemans Bin 65 Chardonnay.

PLANK SALMON-SALAD SANDWICHES

1	regular cedar plank, soaked in water for at least 1 hour	1
1 lb	My Original Cedar-Planked Salmon (p. 89), chilled	500 g
1	medium red onion, finely diced	1
1	lemon, juiced	1
8 oz	brick-style cream cheese, softened	250 g
1 Tbsp	chopped fresh dill	15 mL
	Salt and pepper, to taste	
12	slices marble rye bread	12
2 Tbsp	soft butter	30 mL

GARNISHES:

2	bunches fresh arugula, washed and patted dry	2
1	red onion, thinly sliced	1
1	seedless cucumber, thinly sliced	1

This is a great recipe to make with freshly planked salmon, but I like to use it with leftover plank salmon. Great way to use up those "must goes."

• Flake salmon into a medium bowl. Gently blend in red onion, lemon juice, cream cheese and dill. Season with salt and pepper to taste. Butter each slice of bread on one side.

• Spread equal amounts of plank salmon salad on buttered side of 6 slices of bread.

• Top 6 slices of bread with arugula, red onion and cucumber. Place other salmon salad—coated rye bread on top of cucumber, salmon side down; press gently. Cut in half on the bias and serve.

• Serve with Lindemans Bin 85 Pinot Grigio.

SERVES 6

THE REAL POOR BOY—POOR BOY SANDWICH

1	6-inch (15 cm) regular cedar plank, soaked in water	1
1	can (12 oz/375 g) SPAM	1
¼ cup	thinly sliced red onion	60 mL
¼ cup	sliced green olives	60 mL
¼ cup	thinly sliced gherkins	60 mL
2 Tbsp	honey mustard	30 mL
2	8-inch (20 cm) long soft white sub rolls, sliced in half lengthways	2
2 Tbsp	mayonnaise	30 mL
2 cups	shredded iceberg lettuce	500 mL
8	thin tomato slices	8

That's right people; I even plank SPAM—I told you, you can plank anything! Quick fact: The wonderful state of Hawaii sells more SPAM than anywhere else in the USA.

• Preheat grill to medium heat. Open tin of SPAM, tip if upside down and give it a good shake to loosen from the tin. Slice SPAM in half. Place both halves on plank. Place plank on grill and close lid. Plank bake for 15 to 20 minutes until the SPAM is a little crisp on the outside and heated through.

• Meanwhile, in a small bowl, combine the red onion, green olives, gherkins and honey mustard; set aside. Remove SPAM from grill. Slice each half of the planked SPAM into 8 slices. Brush the bottom half of each bun with mayonnaise. Top each half with shredded lettuce and 4 slices of tomato. Arrange the planked SPAM slices on top of the tomatoes. Spoon the red onion mixture evenly over top of each sandwich. Top with bun lid and serve immediately.

SERVES 2 TO 4

SUCCULICIOUS SIDES

FIRE-ROASTED HICKORY-PLANKED BBQ SAUCE

2	regular hickory planks, soaked in water	2
12	Roma tomatoes, cores removed	12
4	red peppers, halved lengthwise and seeded	4
4	red hot chili peppers (e.g. red jalapeno or finger)	4
2	large onions, halved lengthwise	2
¼ cup	balsamic vinegar	60 mL
2 Tbsp	Bone Dust BBQ Seasoning (p. 46)	30 mL
2 Tbsp	olive oil	30 mL
1½ cups	Sleeman Honey Brown Lager	375 mL
1 cup	brown sugar	250 mL
1 cup	ketchup	250 mL
½ cup	cider vinegar	125 mL
¼ cup	Worcestershire sauce	60 mL
¼ cup	maple syrup	60 mL
2 Tbsp	chopped garlic	30 mL
	Salt and freshly ground black pepper	

This is a great all-purpose BBQ sauce. The initial work of smoking the ingredients will give the sauce a natural smoke flavor that can be added to ribs, steaks, burgers, salmon and chops when time doesn't permit plank grilling.

• Preheat grill to medium-high heat. Toss the tomatoes, red peppers, hot peppers and onions with the balsamic vinegar, Bone Dust BBQ Seasoning and olive oil.

• Reserving the leftover marinade, remove the tomatoes, peppers and onions from the bowl and arrange on the planks.

• Place planks on grill and close lid. Plank grill for 30 to 40 minutes, until the vegetables are slightly tender and lightly charred. Remove from grill and set aside to cool.

• Coarsely chop the planked vegetables. Transfer to a large pot. Add the beer, brown sugar, ketchup, vinegar, Worcestershire sauce, maple syrup, chopped garlic and reserved marinade. Stir to combine. Bring to a boil over medium-high heat. Reduce heat to medium-low and simmer for 45 minutes. Purée in a blender; strain through a fine sieve, season with salt and pepper, and cool.

MAKES ABOUT 8 CUPS (2 L)

CEDAR-PLANKED WHITE CHEDDAR MASHED POTATOES

1	regular cedar plank, soaked in water	1
2 lbs	Yukon Gold potatoes	1 kg
4	cloves garlic, minced	4
1	small onion, sliced	1
1 tsp	salt	5 mL
6 Tbsp	butter	90 mL
¼ cup	whipping cream	60 mL
¼ cup	sour cream	60 mL
4	cheese strings, cut into ½-inch (1 cm) chunks	4
½ cup	grated white Cheddar cheese	125 mL
2 Tbsp	chopped fresh parsley	30 mL
	Salt and pepper	
	Butter	

Mash until fluffy and smooth or leave them a little lumpy. These are your taters, so make 'em how you like! Remember, mashed potatoes plank cook best when they are a day old, so use this recipe when you need to make some of the meal ahead.

• Place potatoes in a large pot and cover with cold water. Add garlic, onions and salt and bring to a boil over high heat. Reduce heat to medium-low and simmer for 20 to 30 minutes or until potatoes are fully cooked and tender. Drain and return pan to heat. Shake pan to remove excess moisture from potatoes, garlic and onions. Remove from heat.

• Mash potatoes, garlic and onion using a potato masher. Add butter, cream and sour cream to mashed potatoes; stir to combine. Cool for 20 minutes. Stir in cheese string pieces, white Cheddar and parsley. Season with salt and pepper to taste; mix well. Transfer to a large bowl and cool completely. Cover and refrigerate for 24 hours.

• Mound the cold potatoes onto the plank. Firmly pat and smooth evenly. Alternatively, scoop the cold potatoes with an ice cream scoop to make small, individual mounds. (It's a little more formal than the family-style mound, so have it your way.)

• Preheat grill to medium-high heat. Place plank on grill and close lid. Plank bake for 20 to 25 minutes, until the potatoes are golden brown and crisp on the outside and hot all the way through. Carefully remove plank from grill and serve potatoes topped with extra butter.

SERVES 8

VARIATIONS: This recipe for mashed potatoes can be used for many different combinations. Mound 'em high on a plank plain or mix lobster and Brie or bacon and Cheddar cheese into the mashed potatoes before planking.

PLANK-SMOKED BACON BAKED BEANS

1	Plank Roasting Pan (p. 36), soaked in water	1
2 Tbsp	olive oil	30 mL
4	cloves garlic, minced	4
3	jalapeno peppers, diced	3
1	large onion, diced	1
3	cans (14 oz/398 mL each) white kidney beans	3
1 cup	diced Plank-Smoked Bacon (p. 207)	250 mL
1 cup	ketchup	250 mL
½ cup	loosely packed brown sugar	125 mL
½ cup	Ted Reader's World Famous Beerlicious BBQ Sauce or your favorite smoky-style BBQ sauce	125 mL
¼ cup	Jack Daniel's Whiskey	60 mL
2 Tbsp	Dijon mustard	30 mL
1 Tbsp	Worcestershire sauce	15 mL
1 tsp	hot pepper sauce	5 mL
	Bone Dust BBQ Seasoning (p. 46)	
	Salt	
1 lb	thick-sliced bacon (approximately 12 slices)	500 g

• Heat the oil in a skillet set over medium-high heat. Add the garlic, jalapeno peppers and onion. Cook for 2 to 3 minutes, until tender. Transfer to a large bowl. Add white kidney beans, diced bacon, ketchup, brown sugar, BBQ sauce, Jack Daniel's, mustard, Worcestershire sauce and hot sauce to the onion mixture. Add Bone Dust BBQ Seasoning and salt to taste; mix well. Transfer to Plank Roasting Pan.

• Preheat grill to medium heat. Twist each piece of bacon to resemble a corkscrew and spread out over the bean mixture. Cover pan loosely with aluminum foil. Place plank roasting pan on grill and close lid. Plank roast for 30 minutes, checking the box periodically to see that it has not ignited.

• Remove aluminum foil and continue to plank bake the beans for another 45 to 60 minutes, until beans are hot and bubbly.

SERVES 8 TO 10

PLANK BOX STUFFING

1	Plank Roasting Pan (p. 36), soaked in water	1
12 cups	white bread, 1½–2-inch (4–5 cm) cubes	3 L
½ cup	chopped fresh herbs, such as savory, sage, thyme and parsley	125 mL
2 Tbsp	Seafood Plank Seasoning (p. 45)	30 mL
6 Tbsp	butter, cut in large cubes, divided	90 mL
3	ribs celery, finely diced	3
2	medium onions, finely diced	2
½ lb	thick-sliced, double-smoked bacon, chopped	250 g
½ lb	smoked ham, chopped	250 g
½ cup	milk	125 mL
	Salt and freshly ground black pepper	

This smoke-kissed stuffing is perfect when paired with the Plank-Smoked Turkey (p. 143).

• In a large bowl, combine the bread cubes, fresh herbs and Seafood Plank Seasoning; set aside.

• Melt 2 Tbsp (30 mL) of butter in a saucepan set over medium heat. Add the celery and onions and sauté, stirring frequently, for 3 to 4 minutes, until softened. Add the bacon and smoked ham and continue to sauté for 5 to 6 minutes, until lightly browned.

• Add remaining butter and the milk to the pan; reduce the temperature to medium-low. Heat until the butter has melted but do not boil. Pour over the bread, season with salt and pepper and mix well.

• Preheat grill to medium-high heat. Transfer bread mixture to the Plank Roasting Pan, packing the mixture evenly into the corners and sides.

• Place stuffing-filled box on the grill; close lid and plank roast for 20 to 30 minutes, until golden brown on top and heated through. Remove from grill and serve with Plank-Smoked Turkey (p. 143).

SERVES 8 TO 12

PLANKED ROOT VEGETABLE HAYSTACKS

1	thin alder plank, soaked in water	1
4	parsnips, peeled and trimmed	4
4	carrots, peeled and trimmed	4
1	celery root, peeled	1
1	large white onion	1
¼ cup	unsalted butter, divided	60 mL
2	cloves garlic, minced	2
2 Tbsp	fresh herbs, chopped	30 mL
2 Tbsp	Seafood Plank Seasoning (p. 45)	30 mL
½ cup	white wine	125 mL
	Salt and freshly ground black pepper	

• Preheat grill to medium heat. Cut parsnips, carrots, celery root and onion into ½-inch (1 cm) thick slices, about 4-inches (10 cm) long.

• Melt 2 Tbsp (30 mL) butter in a medium-sized foil pan and add parsnips, carrots, celery root and onions. Place pan on heated grill. Sauté vegetables for 2 to 3 minutes or until they begin to soften. Add garlic, herbs and Seafood Plank Seasoning and mix well to combine. Pour white wine into pan and continue to cook vegetables until most of the liquid has evaporated.

• Remove pan from grill and drain excess liquid into a small saucepan. Add 2 Tbsp (30 mL) of butter to saucepan and whisk until butter is melted and incorporated into wine mixture. Season with salt and pepper; keep warm.

• Season vegetables with salt and pepper to taste; mix well. Make one large pile of vegetables on the plank. Place plank on grill and close lid. Plank grill vegetables for 10 to 12 minutes, until vegetables are golden brown and hot throughout. Drizzle with warm butter and wine mixture.

SERVES 6

PLANKED STUFFED SWEET ONIONS

2	thin maple planks, soaked in water	2
6	large, unpeeled white onions	6
3 cups	Sleeman No. 20	750 mL
1 Tbsp	Seafood Plank Seasoning (p. 45)	15 mL
½ cup	shredded mozzarella cheese	125 mL
¼ cup	grated Parmesan cheese	60 mL
½ cup	Japanese panko bread crumbs	125 mL
4	slices double smoked bacon, cooked until crisp and coarsely chopped	4
2 Tbsp	fresh parsley, chopped	30 mL
1 tsp	Bone Dust BBQ Seasoning (p. 46)	5 mL
6	small, fresh bocconcini cheese balls	6
	Salt and pepper	

Nothing beats the flavor of sweet onions, except maybe when they're planked! This recipe is sweeter still because you'll never shed a tear over these onions. Serve these with your favorite steak.

• Wash unpeeled onions under cold water to remove any grit. Pat onions dry with paper towel. Peel away loose onion skin. Lightly trim tops of onions to remove stem. Lightly trim root end of onion but don't remove too much as this is what holds the layers of an onion together.

• Place cleaned and trimmed onions into a large stock pot filled with beer and enough water to cover the onions by 1 inch (2.5 cm). Bring mixture to a rolling boil; reduce heat to medium-low and simmer onions for 30 minutes, until just tender.

• Allow onions to cool in poaching liquid. (This may take a few hours.) Drain onions, discarding poaching liquid. Place onions in a bowl; cover and refrigerate for 1 hour or for up to 24 hours.

• Use a sharp paring knife to trim the root end from each onion so that it will stand upright. Next, pierce each onion at a 45° angle about 1-inch (2.5 cm) below the top of the onion. Push the paring knife into the onion until the tip reaches the center of the onion. Cut in a circular motion to hollow out the center of the onion to make a crater in the top; peel skin from onions. Make the crater as deep as possible without cutting through the base of the onion. Chop removed onion tops; set aside. Evenly space hollowed onions on the planks; set aside.

• Combine diced poached onion, mozzarella, Parmesan cheese, panko crumbs, bacon, parsley, and Bone Dust BBQ Seasoning until well combined.

• Preheat grill to medium heat. Place one ball of bocconcini cheese into the cavity of each onion and season with salt and pepper to taste. Mound the cheese stuffing on top of the bocconcini, pressing firmly to fill each onion snugly.

• Place plank on grill and close lid. Plank grill for 30 to 40 minutes, until onions are golden brown and the stuffing is hot and crispy. Remove from grill.

• Serve with Sleeman No. 20 Anniversary.

MAKES 6

PLANKED BEET SALAD

1	regular cedar plank, soaked in water	1
4	medium beets	4
1 Tbsp	olive oil	15 mL
	Salt and pepper	

DRESSING:

¼ cup	olive oil	60 mL
2 Tbsp	Dijon mustard	30 mL
2 Tbsp	whole-grain mustard	30 mL
1 Tbsp	white wine or tarragon vinegar	15 mL
1	large Vidalia or sweet onion, sliced into ½-inch (1 cm) rounds	1
¼ cup	maple syrup	60 mL
1½ tsp	chopped fresh thyme	7 mL
4 cups	arugula	1 L
½ cup	crumbled goat cheese	125 mL

• Preheat grill to medium heat. Rub the beets with the olive oil and salt and pepper to taste. Place on the grill over indirect heat. Close the lid and roast for 45 minutes to 1 hour, until almost fork tender. Remove from heat and cool completely. Peel the beets, discarding skin, and slice into ½-inch (1 cm) thick slices; set aside.

DRESSING: Combine the olive oil, Dijon mustard, whole-grain mustard and vinegar. Mix well and season with salt and pepper to taste; set aside.

• Toss the beet slices and onion rounds with the maple syrup and fresh thyme, season with salt and pepper to taste.

• Preheat grill to medium-high heat. Arrange the beet slices and onion evenly on a plank. Place plank on grill and close lid. Plank roast for 15 to 20 minutes. Remove plank from grill and cool to room temperature.

• Arrange an equal amount of arugula on each of 4 plates. Arrange beets and onion over arugula. Drizzle liberally with mustard dressing and sprinkle with crumbled goat cheese.

SERVES 4

PLANKED BOCCONCINI AND TOMATO BREAD SALAD

1	18-inch (45 cm) x 8-inch (20 cm) regular cedar plank, soaked in water	1

BREAD:

½	multigrain or plain baguette	½
3 Tbsp	olive oil	45 mL
2	cloves garlic, minced	2
2 Tbsp	chopped fresh herbs, such as basil and parsley	30 mL
	Coarsely ground black pepper	
	Coarse sea salt	

VEGETABLES:

1	Vidalia onion, peeled and cut in half	1
1	sweet pepper, halved, stem removed	1
1 tsp	olive oil	5 mL
¼ cup	chopped fresh herbs, such as basil and parsley	60 mL
1 Tbsp	coarsely ground black pepper	15 mL
1 Tbsp	coarse sea salt	15 mL
24	baby bocconcini balls, drained	24
24	large cherry tomatoes	24
3 Tbsp	olive oil	45 mL
2 Tbsp	balsamic vinegar	30 mL
	Fresh basil leaves	

Select the "cocktail" size bocconcini balls for this recipe. They fit perfectly into a hollowed-out cherry tomato. As they cook on the plank, the cheese orbs will get hot, soft and gooey to create an explosion in your mouth; it's orgasmic!

BREAD: Preheat grill to medium heat. Cut baguette into ½-inch (1 cm) cubes and place into a foil pan. Drizzle bread with olive oil and toss with garlic, fresh herbs, and salt and pepper to taste until evenly coated. Place pan into grill and close lid. Toast bread, tossing every few minutes so that bread toasts evenly, until dry and very light golden brown. Remove pan from grill; set aside.

VEGETABLES: Drizzle onion and pepper with olive oil and season with salt and pepper to taste. Place onion and pepper onto grill and cook for 3 to 4 minutes per side, until lightly charred and tender. Remove from grill and cool slightly. Slice onion and pepper into ½-inch (1 cm) wide strips. Add sliced onion to the toasted bread and toss to combine well. Set aside peppers.

• In a medium bowl, combine chopped fresh herbs, coarsely ground black pepper, and sea salt. Add bocconcini to bowl and toss until cheese is evenly coated; set aside.

• Slice bottom from each tomato, leaving the stem end intact. Using a very small spoon or knife, carefully scoop out the middle of each tomato (the seeds and some of the core) to create a cup. Place each tomato cup, stem end down, on a flat surface and gently press one bocconcini ball into each hollowed-out tomato; set aside.

• Place stuffed tomatoes onto center of plank, ensuring each tomato stands upright. Place sliced sweet pepper in a pile on one side of the stuffed tomatoes, and place a pile of bread and onions on the opposite side of the tomatoes.

• Place plank on grill and close lid. Plank grill bread salad for 10 to 15 minutes, until cheese is melted and light golden brown and bread cubes are golden brown and crisp. Remove plank from grill. In a large bowl, toss peppers with onions and toasted bread. Drizzle with olive oil and balsamic vinegar and toss to coat well. Arrange mixture on a platter and scatter stuffed tomatoes and fresh basil leaves on top. Serve immediately.

• Serve with Lindemans Bin 85 Pinot Grigio.

SERVES 4 TO 6

PLANKED BREAKFAST STRATA

1	Plank Roasting Pan (p. 36), soaked in water	1
½	Planked Mashed Potatoes (p. 174)	½
2 cups	shredded mozzarella cheese	500 mL
1 cup	Velveeta cheese, diced	250 mL
1 cup	diced, cooked double-smoked bacon	250 mL
1 cup	frozen spinach, thawed, drained, squeezed of excess moisture, and chopped	250 mL
	Salt and pepper	
8	large eggs	8
2½ cups	whipping cream	625 mL
2 Tbsp	Bone Dust BBQ Seasoning (p. 46)	30 mL

This planking recipe requires a bit of work but will make a believer out of even non-breakfast people. The keys are to use my Plank Roasting Pan (p. 36) and day-old mashed potatoes. It's similar to a crustless quiche. Plank bake it and dig in. It's a big breakfast that goes great with toast, coffee and a beer.

• Preheat grill to medium heat. Line the Plank Roasting Pan with the day-old mashed potatoes, pressing them evenly into all the corners and edges, leaving a large, rectangular well in the center (it will look like a really thick pie crust).

• Toss the mozzarella with the Velveeta cheese, bacon and spinach until well combined and add salt and pepper to taste. Spread the bacon-spinach-cheese mixture evenly into the potato-lined roasting pan.

• Whisk the eggs, cream and Bone Dust BBQ Seasoning together until frothy and fully combined.

• Place the Plank Roasting Pan into the grill, and pour the egg mixture evenly over the spinach, bacon and cheese. Fill as much as you can without overflowing. Close the lid of the grill and plank roast for 1 hour; check occasionally for flare-ups caused by overflowing. Should flare-ups become an issue, turn off one burner and move the roasting pan to cook over indirect heat.

SERVES 8 TO 10

MARTY'S BREAKFAST SAUSAGE BAKE

1	regular hardwood maple plank, soaked in water	1
6 cups	Cedar-Planked White Cheddar Mashed Potatoes (p. 228), prepared the night before	1.5 L
1	green onion, minced	1
1 cup	shredded aged white Cheddar cheese	250 mL
24	breakfast sausages	24
½ cup	warmed maple syrup	125 mL

The butter tarts my friend Marty Curtis makes at his restaurant in Bracebridge, Ontario, Canada are World Famous. They really are to die for! Marty loves food as much as I do, but when I asked him for a recipe for this book he was a bit unsure about what to make. When he said he was thinking of some kind of planked breakfast sausage bake where the sausages were built up like a house, I thought he was a bit crazy. Then, I figured, "Why not?" So here is your breakfast sausage bake, "à la Marty Curtis."

• In the morning, remove mashed potatoes from refrigerator and transfer to a large bowl. Stir in the green onions and Cheddar cheese. Mound the mashed potatoes onto the plank in a pyramid shape that is the length of the plank. Press the breakfast sausages into the mashed potatoes to form a pattern that looks like the roof of a log cabin.

• Preheat grill to medium heat. Place plank on grill and close lid. Plank grill for 20 to 30 minutes, rotating each of the sausages halfway through planking, until the mashed potatoes are warmed through and the sausages are fully cooked and slightly crisp. Remove from grill and drizzle with warm maple syrup. Serve immediately with fried or scrambled eggs, toast, jam and a great cup of coffee.

SERVES 6

PLANKED SPAGHETTI AND MEATBALLS

1	regular cedar plank, soaked in water	1

MEATBALLS:

4	slices Calabrese-style bread	4
½ cup	milk	125 mL
2 lb	ground veal	1 kg
½ lb	ground pork	250 g
8	cloves garlic, minced	8
1	large onion, finely diced	1
	Salt and pepper	
	Nonstick cooking spray	

SPAGHETTI:

1 Tbsp	salt	15 mL
1	pkg. (1 lb/500 g) spaghetti	1
4 cups	Spicy Tomato Sauce (p. 81)	1 L
1 cup	torn, fresh basil leaves	250 mL
2 Tbsp	olive oil	30 mL
¼ cup	grated Romano cheese (approx.)	60 mL
	Chili flakes	

• In a bowl, combine sliced Calabrese bread and milk. Soak for 10 to 15 minutes, until the bread is soft and a little mushy.

• In a large bowl, combine the ground veal and pork, garlic, onion, salt and pepper. Add the soaked bread, squeezing the milk from the bread, before adding. Discard milk. Using your hands, mix the meat mixture well to incorporate ingredients. Refrigerate meat mixture for 30 minutes to allow the flavors to meld.

• Remove meat from refrigerator and form into balls, about 3 oz (90 g) each. Place meatballs onto a parchment paper or foil-lined baking tray and refrigerate for another 30 minutes, allowing the meatballs to set.

• Preheat grill to medium-high heat. Place meatballs evenly spaced on plank and spray with nonstick cooking spray. Place plank on grill and close lid. Plank bake for 15 to 20 minutes, until meatballs are fully cooked but still moist and juicy. The internal temperature of the meatballs should register 170°F (85°C) on an instant-read thermometer.

SPAGHETTI: Meanwhile, bring a large pot of water to a rapid boil. Add salt. Add spaghetti and stir so that it doesn't stick to itself or the pan. Return to boil and cook for about 10 minutes, stirring occasionally, until the pasta is al dente. Drain. After adding the pasta to the boiling water, heat the tomato sauce in another saucepan.

• Toss hot pasta with basil, olive oil, Romano cheese and season with salt and pepper to taste. Transfer to a serving bowl. Add sauce and meatballs. Top with freshly grated Romano cheese and chili flakes.

SERVES 6 TO 8

TIP: To ensure you've added enough salt and pepper to the meat mixture, cook a spoonful of the mixture in the microwave; taste and then add more salt and pepper if necessary to the raw ingredients.

PLANK MAC AND CHEESE BAKE

1	Plank Roasting Pan (p. 36), soaked in water	1
1 lb	double elbow macaroni	500 g
3 Tbsp	butter	45 mL
1	small onion, diced	1
¼ cup	flour	60 mL
2½ cups	milk	625 mL
1 cup	whipping cream	250 mL
2 cups	grated mozzarella cheese	500 mL
2 cups	grated white Cheddar cheese	500 mL
2 tsp	Bone Dust BBQ Seasoning (p. 46)	10 mL
	Salt and pepper to taste	
	Nonstick cooking spray	
	aluminum foil	

• Cook the macaroni in boiling, salted water until it is barely tender. Drain and let cool. In a large saucepan set over medium-low heat, melt the butter. Sauté the onion for 2 to 3 minutes, until translucent and tender. Stir in the flour and blend until incorporated. Slowly pour in the milk and cream, stirring constantly, until the mixture is smooth.

• Continue cooking over medium-low heat, stirring frequently, until thickened, about 10 to 15 minutes. Whisk in the mozzarella and Cheddar cheese until smooth. Remove from heat; add Bone Dust BBQ Seasoning and add salt and pepper to taste; cool slightly. Preheat grill to medium heat.

• In a large bowl, combine cooked pasta with cheese sauce. Mix well to evenly coat the pasta with the sauce. Spray the Plank Roasting Pan with nonstick cooking spray. Pour pasta mixture into plank roasting pan.

• Place plank roasting pan on grill; cover loosely with aluminum foil and close lid. Plank bake for 50 to 60 minutes, until heated through and the top is bubbling. Remove from oven and let rest for 10 minutes before serving.

SERVES 8

PLANK BOX RIGATONI

1	Plank Roasting Pan (p. 36), soaked in water	1
1 Tbsp	salt	15 mL
¼ cup	olive oil, divided	60 mL
5 cups	uncooked rigatoni pasta	1.25 L
1½ lb	ground beef	750 g
2 Tbsp	Bone Dust BBQ Seasoning (p. 46)	30 mL
8 cups	Spicy Tomato Sauce, (p. 81), divided	2 L
2 cups	shredded Fontina cheese	500 mL

TOPPING:

2	large eggs, beaten	2
1 cup	ricotta cheese	250 mL
1 cup	grated Fontina cheese	250 mL
¾ cup	whipping cream	175 mL
1 Tbsp	chopped fresh herbs, such as basil and oregano	15 mL
	Salt and pepper	

• Bring a large pot of water to a rolling boil and add salt and 1 Tbsp (15 mL) of the oil. Add pasta and stir until water returns to a boil. Cook for 8 to 10 minutes, stirring occasionally, until the pasta is al dente (tender but with a firm bite). Drain and set aside.

• In a large frying pan, heat 3 Tbsp (45 mL) of oil over high heat. Add beef and Bone Dust BBQ Seasoning; cook until browned all over. Drain excess moisture and transfer beef to a large bowl; set aside. Add 2 cups (500 mL) of tomato sauce to the same frying pan. Bring sauce to a boil and simmer for 5 minutes. Remove from heat; set aside.

• Add the cooked rigatoni, Fontina cheese and remaining tomato sauce to the bowl with the ground beef; mix well. The mixture should be moist but not very runny. Add a little extra tomato sauce if the mixture looks too dry. Transfer mixture into Plank Roasting Pan. Preheat grill to medium heat.

TOPPING: In a bowl, combine eggs, ricotta cheese, grated Fontina cheese, cream and herbs. Season with salt and pepper to taste, whisk until smooth. Spread evenly over rigatoni mixture.

• Place on grill; cover loosely with aluminum foil and close lid. Plank bake for 45 to 60 minutes, removing the foil halfway through cooking, until the top is golden brown and set and the pasta is hot. Make sure you check the grill periodically to ensure that the plank box has not caught fire. Remove from grill. Rest for 5 to 10 minutes.

SERVES 8

POLENTA ON THE BOARD

1	regular cedar plank, soaked in water	1
4	Roma tomatoes, halved	4
1	large sweet onion, cut into ½-inch (1 cm) rings	1
1	zucchini, thinly sliced lengthways	1
1 Tbsp	Bone Dust Seasoning (p. 46)	15 mL
1 Tbsp	olive oil	15 mL
½ cup	tomato sauce	125 mL
2 cups	chicken stock	500 mL
1 tsp	salt	5 mL
1 cup	cornmeal	250 mL
2 Tbsp	butter	30 mL
½ cup	grated Parmesan cheese	125 mL
	Salt and pepper	
1 cup	crumbled Gorgonzola cheese	250 mL

• Preheat grill to medium-high heat. Season tomatoes, onion and zucchini with Bone Dust BBQ Seasoning and toss with olive oil. Grill vegetables for 4 to 5 minutes, turning once, until lightly charred and tender. Remove from grill and cool slightly.

• Meanwhile, heat tomato sauce in a small saucepan set over medium heat. Reduce heat to very low and keep warm until needed.

• In a large saucepan, bring the chicken stock to a boil over high heat; add 1 tsp (5 mL) salt. Reduce heat to medium-low and add cornmeal in a steady stream while whisking constantly. Using a wooden spoon, stir constantly for 15 to 20 minutes, until cornmeal is thick and smooth. Remove from heat.

• Stir in the butter and Parmesan cheese until smooth. Season polenta with salt and pepper to taste. Let cool in the pot for about 5 minutes. Preheat grill to high heat.

• Spoon cooled polenta onto the cedar plank, piling it high and leaving a 1-inch (2.5 cm) border around the edge of the plank. Make a little well in the center of the polenta and spoon tomato sauce into well. Arrange vegetables on top of tomato sauce and top with crumbled Gorgonzola cheese.

• Place plank on the center of the grill and close the lid. Bake for 10 to 15 minutes, until the polenta is lightly browned and hot and cheese is melted. Remove from the grill and serve immediately.

SERVES 4 TO 6

GRILLED VEGETABLE PLANKZAGNA

1	regular cedar plank, soaked in water	1
1	Plank Roasting Pan (p. 36), soaked in water	1

WHITE SAUCE:

¾ lb	provolone cheese	375 g
¾ lb	mozzarella cheese	375 g
3 Tbsp	butter	45 mL
1	small onion, diced	1
¼ cup	all-purpose flour	60 mL
1½ cups	milk	375 mL
1 cup	whipping cream	250 mL
1 tsp	paprika	5 mL
1 tsp	dry mustard	5 mL
	Salt and freshly ground black pepper	
2 cups	soft unripened ricotta, drained	500 mL
3 cups	mozzarella cheese, shredded	750 mL
1½ cups	grated Parmesan cheese	375 mL
¼ cup	fresh parsley, chopped	60 mL
4	portobello mushrooms, soaked in water	4
4	zucchini, sliced lengthwise into ⅛-inch (3 mm) strips	4
2	large red bell peppers	2
2	onions, sliced into ⅛-inch (3 mm) rings	2
2 Tbsp	olive oil	30 mL
2 Tbsp	Seafood Plank Seasoning (p. 45)	30 mL
	Nonstick cooking spray	
6	sheets fresh pasta aluminum foil	6

• Place the provolone and mozzarella cheeses into the freezer for a minimum of 1 hour. Preheat grill to medium heat. Place a sheet of nonstick foil or lightly oiled regular foil onto the plank. Fold the sides up to create a ½-inch (1 cm) lip all the way around to create a foil pan the same size as the plank. **NOTE:** This will keep the cheese contained, if it starts to melt.

• Place the frozen cheeses onto the foil-lined plank. Place plank on the grill and close the lid. Plank grill for 15 to 20 minutes. Discard the plank and put the cheeses, still on the foil, into the fridge and chill completely. Remove the cheeses from the foil and coarsely grate; set aside.

• Meanwhile, prepare the white sauce. Melt the butter in a large saucepan over medium-low heat. Sauté the diced onion for 2 to 3 minutes, until transparent and tender. Stir in the flour until incorporated. Slowly pour in the milk and cream, stirring constantly, until the mixture is smooth. Cook, stirring frequently, for 10 to 15 minutes until sauce is thickened.

• Whisk in the smoked, coarsely grated cheeses until smooth. Remove from heat and whisk in paprika and mustard. Season with salt and freshly ground black pepper to taste. Pour sauce into a large mixing bowl and set aside to cool completely. To the cooled plank-smoked cheese sauce, add ricotta, 1 cup (250 mL) shredded, unsmoked mozzarella, ½ cup (125 mL) Parmesan and parsley.

• Preheat grill to medium heat. Remove mushrooms from water and drain on paper towels. Brush mushrooms, sliced zucchini, peppers and onion rings with olive oil and season with Seafood Plank Seasoning. Grill vegetables, turning occasionally, for 6 to 8 minutes, until lightly charred and tender. Remove from grill and cool.

• Slice mushrooms into ¼-inch (5 mm) strips; set aside. Peel and seed grilled red peppers and cut into ½-inch (1 cm) strips.

• Place Plank Roasting Pan onto a flat surface. Spray bottom of plank roasting pan with nonstick cooking spray. Lay 2 pasta sheets over the bottom of the pan; top with zucchini strips, overlapping slightly until pasta sheet is covered. Next, layer with sliced onions, grilled peppers and sliced mushrooms.

- Pour a thin layer of the plank-smoked cheese sauce mixture evenly over the vegetables; sprinkle with some of the remaining mozzarella and Parmesan. Lightly press layers down with a spatula. Repeat layers starting with pasta, until the box is almost full, ending with a layer of plank-smoked cheese sauce mixture, mozzarella and Parmesan. Cover and refrigerate Plankzagna for at least 1 hour to set.

- Preheat grill to medium heat. Place Plank Roasting Pan, uncovered, on grill and close lid. Plank roast Plankzagna for 10 to 15 minutes, checking occasionally that the pan hasn't ignited. If the pan is leaking, remove from grill and wrap bottom half of pan in foil. Turn grill to medium-low and continue to cook for an additional 25 to 30 minutes, until Plankzagna is hot throughout and cheese is melted and bubbling.

- Remove Plankzagna from grill and cool for 5 to 10 minutes to allow to set. Cut into squares to serve.

SERVES 6 TO 8

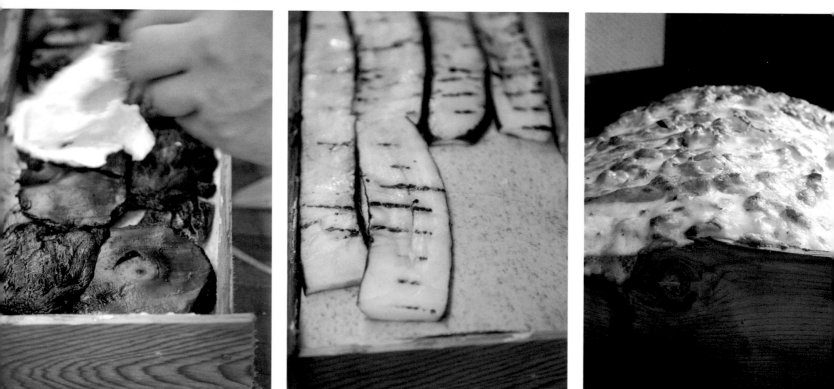

PLANK BAKERY BREADS AND DESSERTS

CARAMELIZED ONION AND HAVARTI PLANKED BISCUITS

1	regular maple or oak or cedar plank, soaked in water	1
2 Tbsp	olive oil	30 mL
1	large sweet onion, thinly sliced	1
1¾ cups	all-purpose flour	425 mL
1 Tbsp	baking powder	15 mL
1 Tbsp	granulated sugar	15 mL
¼ tsp	salt	1 mL
½ cup	cold butter	125 mL
1 cup	finely diced Havarti cheese cubes	250 mL
¾ cup	milk	175 mL
2 Tbsp	chopped fresh dill	30 mL
	Melted butter	

• Heat oil in a frying pan set over medium heat. Add sliced onions and sauté slowly for 30 to 40 minutes, stirring continuously until caramelized, golden brown and very tender. Remove from heat and cool completely. Preheat grill to medium heat.

• Meanwhile, in a large bowl, stir together the flour, baking powder, sugar and salt.

• Using a pastry blender, cut in the butter until the mixture resembles coarse crumbs.

• Make a well in the center. Add the cooled onions, Havarti cheese, milk and dill. Using a wooden spoon, stir just until dry ingredients are moistened.

• Turn out dough onto a lightly floured surface. Knead dough by folding and gently pressing, about 4 to 6 times, just until the dough holds together. Gently pat or press the dough out into a 6-inch (15 cm) square, about 1-inch (2.5 cm) thick. Use a 2-inch (5 cm) pastry ring to cut the dough into 12 rounds. Arrange the raw biscuits evenly spaced on plank.

• Plank bake the biscuits for 15 to 20 minutes, until golden brown, hot and flakey. Brush with melted butter and serve warm.

SERVES 12

PLANK BOX CHEESY JALAPENO CORN BREAD

1	Plank Roasting Pan (p. 36), soaked in water	1
	Nonstick cooking spray	
½ cup	all-purpose flour	125 mL
¾ cup	cornmeal	175 mL
½ cup	corn flour	125 mL
3 Tbsp	baking powder	45 mL
1 tsp	salt	5 mL
1	large egg	1
⅔ cup	homogenized milk	150 mL
⅓ cup	unsalted butter, softened	75 mL
3	jalapeno peppers, finely diced	3
1	small red onion, sliced, sautéed and cooled	1
1 cup	grated pepper jack cheese	250 mL
	Butter	

• Prepare grill for indirect grilling by turning one side of the grill to low heat and the other to high heat. Spray the bottom of the Plank Roasting Pan with nonstick cooking spray.

• In a large bowl, sift together flour, cornmeal, corn flour, baking powder and salt. In a small bowl with a fork, beat together egg, milk and butter. Add jalapeno pepper, red onion and cheese. Mix well to combine.

• Pour egg mixture into flour mixture. Stir just until flour is moistened and pour batter into Plank Roasting Pan. Spread batter evenly into Roasting Pan and place on grill over the side heated to low heat. Plank bake for 30 to 40 minutes, until golden brown and a toothpick inserted into the center of the cornbread pulls out clean. Remove Plank Roasting Pan from grill and allow to cool for 10 minutes. Cut into squares and serve with butter.

SERVES 10 TO 12

PLANKED PIRAGS

3	regular cedar planks, soaked in water	3
5	large eggs	5
1	envelope quick rise dry yeast	1
5 Tbsp	granulated sugar, divided	75 mL
¾ cup	homogenized milk	175 mL
½ cup	unsalted butter	125 mL
1 tsp	salt	5 mL
3½ cups	all-purpose flour, sifted	875 mL
1 lb	thick-sliced, double-smoked bacon, grilled until lightly charred and finely diced	500 g
1	onion, cut into wedges, grilled and finely diced	1
	Fresh ground black pepper	
3	green onions, finely sliced	3
½ cup	sour cream	125 mL

My mom is from Latvia and as a kid no visit from my grandparents was complete without a box full of pirags, a traditional Latvian pastry filled with smoked bacon and diced onions. After a trip to Latvia I thought that if they were plank-baked it would give the pirag an extra delicious hit of smoke. It took quite a few tests, but eventually we got approval from my, oh-so-meticulous mother!

• In a small bowl, whisk together 2 of the eggs and ⅓ cup (75 mL) cold water; set aside. Pour yeast into a small bowl; add ¼ cup (60 mL) warm water and 1 Tbsp (15 mL) of the sugar. Do not stir; set aside for 10 to 15 minutes.

• Pour milk into a small saucepan and heat to a simmer over medium-high heat. Remove from heat and add butter and salt. Whisk until butter is melted; set aside. In a medium bowl, whisk remaining eggs until frothy. Add remaining sugar and continue to whisk for 1 to 2 minutes; set aside. Place flour in a large bowl. Stir milk mixture into flour until just incorporated.

• Form a small well in the middle of the flour mixture. Pour egg and sugar mixture and yeast mixture into well. Using your hands, knead dough until smooth, about 5 to 10 minutes.

• Lightly dust dough with flour so that it does not stick to the bowl. Cover with a clean, damp tea towel (or plastic wrap) and allow dough to rise at room temperature for 90 minutes, or until dough has doubled in size.

• Meanwhile, in a medium bowl, mix together the bacon and onion. Season with pepper to taste. Cover and refrigerate until needed. Preheat grill to high heat.

• When dough has risen, remove towel or plastic wrap. Using your hands, punch dough down so that it is slightly flattened. Remove dough from bowl and place on a floured cutting board. Halve dough and return one half to the bowl. Cover dough in bowl with damp towel or plastic wrap; set aside.

• Using your hands, roll dough into a long strand, about 1–1½-inches (2.5–4 cm) in diameter. Cut dough into 24 1-inch (2.5 cm) pieces.

• Roll each piece of dough into a small ball and flatten out into a circle about 2-inch (5 cm) in diameter. Set aside on floured cutting board and cover with damp towel. Repeat for all remaining pieces.

• Remove towel from dough. Place 1 tsp (5 mL) of bacon filling in the center of one piece. Lightly brush edge of dough with egg/water mixture. Fold dough over, forming a half-moon shape; press edges to seal. Lightly crimp edges with a fork to seal in filling. Repeat with remaining pieces of dough. When all pirags are assembled, lightly brush tops of each with the egg and water mixture. Using a fork, pierce each one once to release steam during cooking.

• Repeat cutting, rolling, and forming for remaining dough.

• Carefully space pirags onto planks, leaving about a ½-inch (1 cm) gap between them. Place planks on grill and close lid. Plank grill pirags for 12 to 15 minutes, until golden brown and crisp. Serve with green onion and sour cream for dipping.

Serve with shots of ice-cold Finlandia Vodka.

MAKES 48

CEDAR-PLANKED DINNER ROLLS WITH BACON AND CHEESY TOPPING TOO!

2	regular cedar planks, soaked in water	2
4–5 cups	all-purpose flour, divided	1–1.25 L
⅓ cup	granulated sugar	75 mL
1½ tsp	salt	7 mL
2	envelopes quick rise dry yeast	2
1 cup	whole milk	250 mL
¼ cup	unsalted butter	60 mL
2	large eggs	2
2 Tbsp	butter, clarified	30 mL
	Kosher salt	

HERB GARLIC BUTTER:

½ cup	butter, softened	125 mL
¼ cup	each chopped fresh thyme and parsley	60 mL
¼ cup	puréed planked-roasted garlic (see Cedar Plank–Roasted Garlic Soup, p. 51)	60 mL
2 Tbsp	Seafood Plank Seasoning (p. 45)	30 mL

• Sift together 1½ cups (325 mL) of the flour, sugar, salt and yeast into the large bowl of a mixer. In a medium saucepan, heat milk and butter until hot, about 120°F (50°C).

• At low speed, using paddle attachment for the mixer, gradually beat milk mixture into dry ingredients. Increase speed of mixer to medium and beat for 2 minutes; occasionally stop mixer and scrape sides and bottom of bowl with a rubber spatula.

• Add eggs and ½ cup (125 mL) more flour and continue to beat for 2 to 3 minutes. Remove bowl from mixer and add 2–2½ cups (500–625 mL) of remaining flour. Using your hands, knead in more flour if dough is wet.

• Remove dough from bowl and place on a lightly floured surface. Knead dough until smooth and elastic, about 10 minutes. Shape dough into a ball. Lightly grease a large bowl with butter. Cover dough ball with a clean damp towel and allow to rise in a warm area, undisturbed, until doubled, about 1 hour.

• Punch down dough, transfer to a lightly floured cutting board, and cut dough in half. Cover with damp towel and allow to rest for 15 minutes.

• Meanwhile, prepare Herb Garlic Butter. In a small bowl, mix together butter, herbs, garlic and Seafood Plank Seasoning. Cover and set aside at room temperature.

• Preheat grill to medium heat. Cut each portion of dough into 8 equal pieces and shape into oval balls, tapering ends slightly. Place dough balls onto planks about 2-inches (5 cm) apart; cover with a clean damp cloth, and allow to rise until doubled, about 30 minutes.

• With a sharp, floured knife, make a lengthwise slash halfway through the center of each roll. Brush rolls lightly with clarified butter and sprinkle with kosher salt. Place planks on grill and close lid. Plank grill for 10 to 12 minutes, until golden brown and cooked throughout. Serve with Herb Garlic Butter on the side.

MAKES 16

PEAR AND BLACKBERRY CRISP

1	Plank Roasting Pan (p. 36) Nonstick cooking spray	1
4 cups	fresh pear, peeled, cored and cut into ½-inch (1 cm) thick slices	4
4 cups	Asian pear, peeled, cored and cut into ½-inch (1 cm) thick slices	4
2 cups	fresh blackberries	500 mL
½ cup	Chambord liqueur	125 mL
¼ cup	Southern Comfort liqueur	60 mL
1 tsp	vanilla extract	5 mL
2 cups	lightly packed brown sugar, divided	500 mL
¼ cup	tapioca starch	60 mL
	Salt	
2 cups	rolled oats	500 mL
½ cup	cold butter, cut into small cubes	125 mL
½ cup	chopped walnuts or pecans	125 mL
	Vanilla ice cream	

• In a large bowl, combine the pear, Asian pear, blackberries, Chambord, Southern Comfort and vanilla. Mix well and macerate for 1 hour. Add 1 cup (250 mL) of the sugar, tapioca starch and a pinch of salt. Mix and set aside.

• Preheat grill to medium-high heat. In a bowl, combine the remaining sugar, rolled oats, butter, walnuts and a pinch of salt. Mix together by rubbing the mixture between your hands until it forms small balls or crumbles; set aside.

• Spray Plank Roasting Pan with nonstick cooking spray. Pour in pear mixture and spread evenly. Sprinkle reserved crumble mixture over top in an even layer.

• Bake for 45 to 60 minutes, until crumble is golden brown and the fruit mixture is bubbling and thick. Cool for 10 to 15 minutes. Serve with vanilla ice cream.

SERVES 8

SOUTHERN COMFORT BAKED APPLES WITH BUTTER ON TOP

1	regular apple wood plank, soaked in apple cider or apple juice	1
4	large, tart baking apples	4
1 cup	Southern Comfort liquer (approx.)	250 mL
1 cup	cold water	250 mL
½ cup	lightly packed brown sugar	125 mL
½ cup	chopped almonds	125 mL
¼ cup	golden sultana raisins	60 mL
1 tsp	ground cinnamon	5 mL
¼ tsp	ground ginger	1 mL
	Vanilla ice cream	

• Core the apples, leaving the bottom ½-inch (1 cm) of the apple intact. Place apples in a large bowl and pour over Southern Comfort and 1 cup (250 mL) of cold water. Cover and refrigerate to allow apples to marinate for 1 to 2 hours. Remove from liquid.

• Mix together the brown sugar, almonds, raisins, cinnamon, ginger and a big splash of additional Southern Comfort. Fill the apples with this sugar mixture.

• Preheat grill to medium heat. Place plank on grill; close lid and heat for 2 to 3 minutes, until plank starts to crackle and smoke. Place stuffed apples, evenly spaced on the preheated plank. Plank bake for 40 to 45 minutes, until the apples are soft and tender but not mushy and the filling is hot and bubbly. Drizzle with a little extra Southern Comfort and serve immediately with vanilla ice cream.

SERVES 4

PLANKIES

1	regular cedar plank, soaked in water	1	
8	Twinkies (4 pkg.)	8	
¾ cup	Nutella (chocolate hazelnut spread)	175 mL	
6	Oreo cookies, smashed into chunks	6	
½ cup	mini marshmallows	125 mL	
¼ cup	chocolate toffee pieces	60 mL	

I was tailgating in Buffalo at a Buffalo Bills game when the inspiration for this recipe hit me. I'm not sure if it was the testosterone overload, the beer, the Jack or the combination of the three, but the crowds loved them. Truly evil decadence! This is proof that anything can be planked!

• Preheat grill to medium-low heat. Arrange the Twinkies on the plank. Slather the top of the Twinkies evenly with Nutella. Sprinkle with mini Oreo chunks, marshmallows and chocolate toffee pieces.

• Place plank on grill and close lid. Allow Twinkies to heat and smoke slowly for 15 minutes, until marshmallows are golden brown and everything is heated through. Remove from grill and serve immediately with a big glass of milk.

SERVES 4 TO 8

PLANKED APPLE CAKE

1	regular western red cedar plank, soaked in water	1
1	Plank Roasting Pan (p. 36), soaked in water	1
	Nonstick cooking spray	
4–6	Granny Smith apples, halved and cored	4–6
1 cup	lightly packed brown sugar	250 mL
1 Tbsp	Gentleman Jack Whiskey	15 mL
¼ tsp	ground nutmeg	1 mL
¼ tsp	ground cinnamon	1 mL
1½ cups	cake and pastry flour, sifted	325 mL
8	large eggs, separated	8
1 cup	granulated sugar	250 mL
	lemon juice	
1	lemon, zested and juiced to give 3 Tbsp of juice	1
½ tsp	salt	2 mL

Shortcut this recipe by using a store-bought white cake mix. It works really well and no one has to know you took a shortcut.

• Preheat grill to medium-high heat. Place apple halves, cut side down, onto the plank. Plank grill apples for 20 to 30 minutes, until the skin is a smoky color and the apples are just tender. Remove plank from grill; cool and thinly slice apples. Place apple slices in a large bowl; add ½ cup (125 mL) of the brown sugar, Gentleman Jack, nutmeg and cinnamon. Toss to mix; set aside.

• Maintain medium-high heat on one side of grill and reduce the other side to low heat. Spray the Plank Roasting Pan liberally with nonstick cooking spray.

• Sift flour; set aside. In a large bowl, beat egg yolks until thick and lemon colored. Gradually add ½ cup (125 mL) granulated sugar, beating thoroughly. Beat in the lemon juice and lemon zest; set aside.

• In a clean, dry mixing bowl, using an electric mixer or a balloon whisk, beat egg whites with salt until they form peaks but are not dry. Fold in remaining granulated sugar and then the yolk mixture. Fold in the flour gently to make a smooth and light batter. Do not overmix.

• Pour cake batter into the prepared Plank Roasting Pan, spreading the batter evenly. Scatter the apple slices over the top and sprinkle the remaining brown sugar evenly over top.

• Place pan over the low heat on the grill and plank bake for 50 to 60 minutes, until a toothpick pulls out clean from the center.

• Don't open the grill lid often, as the heat loss will prevent the cake from rising properly. Remove cake from grill and allow to cool in the Plank Roasting Pan. Slice cake into squares.

SERVES 8 TO 12

TIP: Serve cake with scoops of caramel ice cream drizzled with caramel sauce and fresh raspberries. Of course, a big dollop of whipped cream will help, too.

PLANKED BANANA S'MORES CHEESECAKE

1	Plank Roasting Pan (p. 36), soaked in water	1

CRUST:

3 cups	graham cracker crumbs	750 mL
½ cup	unsalted peanuts, crushed	125 mL
½ cup	butter, melted	125 mL
¼ cup	lightly packed brown sugar	60 mL
Pinch	salt	Pinch

FILLING:

4	medium-ripe bananas, peeled and diced	4
1 cup	mini marshmallows	250 mL
1 cup	semi-sweet chocolate chips	250 mL
1 cup	smooth peanut butter, melted	250 mL
2 lb	whipped cream cheese, room temperature	1 kg
1 lb	sour cream, room temperature	500 g
¼ lb	unsalted butter, room temperature	125 g
1¼ cups	granulated sugar	310 mL
1	fresh vanilla bean (split in half and seeds removed)	1
2 tsp	lemon juice, freshly squeezed	10 mL
2 Tbsp	cornstarch	30 mL
5	large eggs, room temperature	5

• Preheat grill to medium-low. Mix together graham cracker crumbs, peanuts, melted butter, brown sugar and salt. Press mixture into bottom of Plank Roasting Pan to form a ¼-inch (5 mm) thick crust.

• Place pan onto grill and plank roast crust for about 10 to 15 minutes, until crisp. Remove pan from grill and cool; leave grill on.

• Meanwhile, in a mixing bowl, combine sliced bananas, marshmallows and chocolate chips. Add melted peanut butter and stir to combine well. Set aside this s'mores mixture; let cool.

• Using an electric mixer, blend cream cheese, sour cream and butter until smooth. Add sugar, vanilla, lemon juice and cornstarch; beat on medium-high until well blended. Beat in eggs, adding one at a time to ensure the entire mixture is very smooth before adding the next egg.

• Pour mixture into the Plank Roasting Pan. Top batter evenly with reserved s'mores mixture. Place cheesecake onto grill and close lid. Plank bake cheesecake for 45 minutes to 1 hour, until the top is golden brown and gooey but the center of cake is still a little runny.

• Turn off grill and allow cheesecake to cool with grill lid open for 20 minutes. Remove cheesecake from grill and let rest at room temperature for 30 minutes. Cover and refrigerate. Bring cheesecake to room temperature before serving. Slice into 8 portions and serve immediately.

SERVES 8

TIP: To make cutting easier, dip knife into warm water between each slice and wipe clean with a towel.

PLANKED CHOCOLATE CHIP COOKIES

4	regular maple planks, soaked in water	4
2 cups	oatmeal	500 mL
2 cups	all-purpose flour, sifted	500 mL
½ tsp	salt	2 mL
1 tsp	baking powder	5 mL
1 tsp	baking soda	5 mL
1 cup	unsalted butter	250 mL
1½ cups	lightly packed brown sugar	325 mL
½ cup	granulated sugar	125 mL
2	large eggs	2
1 tsp	vanilla extract	5 mL
2 cups	chocolate chips	500 mL
1½ cups	macadamia nuts, coarsely chopped	325 mL
1 cup	chocolate toffee pieces	250 mL
¼ cup	maple syrup, warmed	60 mL

I've always said you can plank anything—here's the proof!

• Preheat grill to medium-high heat. Blend oatmeal in food processor until it is a fine powder. Add flour, salt, baking powder, and baking soda and pulse until well combined; set aside.

• In a large bowl, cream together butter, brown sugar and granulated sugar until pale yellow. Add eggs and vanilla and mix until well combined. Add flour mixture to butter mixture and mix thoroughly until blended. Add chocolate chips, macadamia nuts and chocolate toffee pieces; mix until combined.

• Scoop about 1 tsp (5 mL) of cookie dough and roll into a small ball. Flatten dough ball slightly and place onto plank. Repeat with remaining dough, placing balls about 1-inch (2.5 cm) apart, until planks are full.

• Place planks on grill and close lid. Plank bake cookies for 10 to 12 minutes, until cookies are golden brown and fully cooked. Depending on how many planks fit onto the grill, cookies may have to be baked in batches.

• Using a spatula, remove cookies from planks and place onto wire racks or platter to cool. Drizzle with warmed maple syrup just before serving.

MAKES ABOUT 4 DOZEN COOKIES

PLANK-SMOKED CHOCOLATE BROWNIES
WITH GOOEY MARSHMALLOW TOPPING

1	Plank Roasting Pan (p. 36), soaked in water	1
	Nonstick cooking spray	
1¾ cups	all-purpose flour	425 mL
2 tsp	baking powder	10 mL
1 cup	butter	250 mL
8 oz	unsweetened chocolate, coarsely chopped	250 g
5	large eggs	5
3½ cups	granulated sugar	875 mL
1 Tbsp	vanilla	15 mL
½ tsp	salt	2 mL
1½ cups	semi-sweet chocolate chips	375 mL
1½ cups	peanut butter chips, coarsely chopped	375 mL
1½ cups	peanuts, coarsely chopped	375 mL
2 cups	mini marshmallows	500 mL
	Ice cream	

This is so good it should be illegal: Get sticky with the one you love.

• Spray Plank Roasting Pan with nonstick cooking spray; set aside. Sift together the flour and baking powder. Melt butter and chocolate over low heat, stirring occasionally, in a heavy saucepan. When melted, remove from the heat and cool slightly.

• In a large mixing bowl, beat eggs, sugar, vanilla and salt for 10 minutes at medium speed. Blend in the butter mixture at low speed until just mixed. Don't overbeat. Fold the flour mixture gently into the egg mixture until just blended. Gently stir in 1 cup (250 mL) each of chocolate chips, peanut butter chips and peanuts and ½ cup (125 mL) of the marshmallows.

• Preheat the grill to medium heat. Pour the brownie mixture into the prepared Plank Roasting Pan and gently smooth the top. Place pan on grill and close lid. Plank bake for 40 to 45 minutes, until a toothpick inserted into the batter comes out clean.

• In a bowl, combine remaining chocolate chips, peanut butter chips, peanuts and mini marshmallows. Scatter the marshmallow mixture over the warm Plank Roasting Pan–baked brownies. Reduce grill heat to low. Place pan on grill and warm the brownies until the topping is gooey and marshmallows are golden brown, 5 to 10 minutes. Remove from grill. Allow planked brownies to rest for 10 minutes and serve with ice cream.

SERVES 8

SCHMOKEN A PLANCAKE

1	regular cherry plank, soaked in water	1
2	large eggs, beaten	2
1½ cups	buttermilk	375 mL
¼ cup	melted butter	60 mL
2¼ cups	all-purpose flour	560 mL
1 Tbsp	granulated sugar	15 mL
1 Tbsp	baking powder	15 mL
½ tsp	salt	2 mL
½ cup	butter	125 mL
1 cup	chocolate chips	250 mL

SAUCE:

1 cup	maple syrup (approx.)	250 mL
½ cup	lightly packed brown sugar	125 mL
2	ripe bananas, thinly sliced on the bias	2
¼ cup	butter, cubed (approx.)	60 mL

• Preheat grill to medium heat.

• In a bowl, mix the eggs, buttermilk and melted butter until smooth. In a separate, large bowl, sift together the flour, sugar, baking powder and salt. Add the egg mixture to the flour mixture and whisk until just smooth.

• In a medium nonstick frying pan set over medium heat, melt 1–2 Tbsp (15–30 mL) of the butter. Using a small ladle, spoon the pancake batter into the hot pan, making 4-inch (10 cm) pancakes. Sprinkle pancakes with chocolate chips.

• Cook until the bubbles that form on the top of the pancakes begin to burst. Flip and continue to cook until pancakes are golden brown on the bottom, about 1 to 2 more minutes. Repeat until all the batter is used.

SAUCE: Place the maple syrup and brown sugar into a sauté pan and heat over medium heat, stirring until the brown sugar dissolves. Add the banana slices and continue to stir for an additional 4 to 5 minutes, until the syrup thickens a little. Remove from heat and add the butter cubes. Stir well to incorporate all the butter; set aside.

• Place 3 pancakes down the center of the plank. Spoon a little maple syrup/banana mixture onto each one. Place another pancake on top followed by a little more banana. Repeat until all the pancakes and bananas are used.

• Place the plank into the grill and close the lid. Plank bake for 12 to 15 minutes or until hot throughout. Remove from grill and serve immediately with more syrup and butter if necessary.

SERVES 6

BARBECUE COCKTAILS

STRANGE FROOT WHITE SANGRIA

1	regular western cherry or apple plank, soaked in white wine/water mixture	1
2	Asian Pears, halved and seeded	2
2	pears, halved and seeded, stems removed	2
1	mango, peeled and cut into strips	1
1	orange, sliced	1
1	lemon, sliced	1
1	lime, sliced	1
6 cups	Lindemans Bin 65 Chardonnay, chilled	1.5 L
1	sprig fresh sage	1
2	cans (355 mL each) ginger ale, chilled	2

This recipe honors one my favorite rock-and-roll movies, *Still Crazy*. The band in the film was called Strange Froot. For this fictional group I have created this recipe for white wine sangria (but it is just as great made with red wine). It's the perfect drink for any summer barbecue.

• Preheat grill to medium-high heat. Arrange Asian pears, pears and mango on plank. Place plank on grill and close lid. Plank grill fruit for 15 to 18 minutes, until fruit is just tender and lightly smoky.

• Remove fruit from grill and cool completely. Slice Asian pear and pear halves into 8 or 10 slices each. Cut the mango slices into small chunks; quarter the orange, lemon and lime slices.

• Place sliced fruit into a large glass pitcher. Add sprigs of sage. Pour in chardonnay and the ginger ale; stir. Serve immediately in chilled white wine glasses, including some of the planked fruits in each glass.

SERVES 12

TENNESSEE BLOODY CAESAR

1 slice	pickle	1	
2 Tbsp	Bone Dust BBQ Seasoning (page 46)	30 mL	
	Ice		
2 tsp	prepared hot horseradish	10 mL	
Splash	Worcestershire sauce	Splash	
	hot sauce to taste		
4 oz	Jack Daniel's	120 mL	
6 oz	tomato clam cocktail 360 mL	180 mL	
	salt, pepper and Bone Dust BBQ Seasoning to taste		
2	6 inch skewers	2	

Serve this cocktail with either my Sirloin burger (page 213) or Planked Beef Tenderloin with Smoky Mashed Potatoes (page 174).

• Rim a couple of glasses with a pickle.

• Spoon Bone Dust BBQ Seasoning onto a plate evenly.

• Rim the glasses with bone dust.

• Any combination of any of the following drink garnishes:

• Olives, pickles, watermelon pickles, hot peppers, pepperoncini, spicy green beans, cheese (smoked cheddar, bocconcini, smoked gouda), smoked sausage, poached or grilled shrimp, capers, pickled onions or pickles beets. You choose and create your own salad skewers.

• Fill glasses with ice.

• Add a teaspoon of prepared hot horseradish into each glass.

• Add a splash of Worcestershire sauce and hot sauce.

• Add 2 oz of Jack Daniel's to each glass.

• Fill remainder of the glass with tomato clam cocktail.

• Stir, sip to check for seasoning.

• Season to taste with salt, pepper and Bone Dust BBQ Seasoning.

• Garnish with salad skewer and serve.

SERVES 2

BANANA JACK MILKSHAKE

1	blender	1
4 oz	Jack Daniel's Whiskey	120 mL
1	ripe banana, peeled and coarsely chopped	1
1 cup	chocolate chip vanilla ice cream	250 mL
½ cup	vanilla yogurt	60 mL

Serve this as a dessert on its own or with Banana S'mores Cheecake (page 274).

- Put the Jack Daniel's, banana, ice cream and yogurt in a blender.
- Blend until smooth.
- Pour into milkshake glasses or mugs and serve immediately.

SERVES 2

BLACK ICE MARTINI

2	martini glasses	2
1	martini shaker	1
	Ice	
1 part	Finlandia vodka	1
1 part	ice wine, (some Canadian goodness)	1
½ part	Chambord liquer	½
4	fresh blackberries	4

Serve this drink with Planked Crab Cakes (page 133). On the rocks, or straight up, this martini is pure decadence.

• Place martini glasses in freezer.

• Fill martini shaker with ice.

• Add one part vodka to one part ice wine to a half part Chambord.

• Put cap on martini shaker and shake.

• Remove cap. Strain into chilled martini glasses.

• Garnish each glass with a couple of fresh blackberries.

SERVES 2

EL JIMADOR PALOMA

1	Cajun-style injector syringe	1
6 oz	El Jimador Tequila Reposado	180 mL
4	fresh ruby red grapefruits	4
	Ice	
1 cup	soda water	250 mL
Drizzle	Chambord liqueur	Drizzle

Serve this drink with Planked Chicken Chilliquillas (page 157), Bryn's Grilled Chicken Nachos (page 74), or Stuffed Jalepenos (page 84).

• Take a Cajun style injector syringe and fill the chamber with approximately 1–2 oz (15–30 mL) of tequila.

• Gently push the needle of the injector syringe into the center of one grapefruit. Push the syringe plunger and inject the grapefruit with the entire chamber full of tequila. Repeat with remaining grapefruits.

• Place tequila-injected grapefruits into refrigerator and allow them to marinate for 1 hour so that the grapefruit juices combine with the tequila.

• Remove from refrigerator and cut the marinated grapefruit in half. Using a juicer squeeze as much of the precious juice out of the grapefruit as you can, reserving the juice.

• Fill two glasses equally with the tequila infused grapefruit juice. Add ice and top with soda water. Drizzle each with a little Chambord, garnish with a wedge of grapefruit.

• Drink immediately.

SERVES 2

GENTLEMAN'S ICED COFFEE

2 cups	hot strong coffee	500 mL
2 tsp	brown sugar	10 mL
	Ice	
4 oz	Gentleman Jack Whiskey	120 mL
2 oz	coffee cream	60 mL

Serve this with Surf and Turf Steak Rollups (page 180).

- Brew a pot of strong coffee.

- Sweeten, if desired, 2 cups of strong coffee with brown sugar.

- Set aside to cool.

- Fill 2 large coffee mugs or tumblers with ice.

- Pour 2 ounces of Gentleman Jack into each glass.

- Pour cooled coffee over ice and Gentleman Jack.

- Add an ounce of cream to each glass, stir and serve immediately.

- Repeat as desired.

SERVES 2

SOCO EDIBLE COCKTAIL

¼ cup + ½ cup	Southern Comfort liquer	60 mL + 125 mL
¼ cup	balsamic vinegar	60 mL
1 tsp	sugar	5 mL
1	seedless small watermelon	1
1–2 Tbsp	Sweet Spice Rub (page 48)	15–30 mL
2 Tbsp	chopped fresh mint	30 mL

- In a small saucepan, combine ¼ cup of Southern Comfort, balsamic vinegar and sugar. Bring to a low boil over medium heat, reduce to low, stirring occasionally until mixture forms a thick syrup. Remove from heat and set aside.

- Cut the watermelon into small one or two bite wedges. Lay the watermelon wedges in a single layer in a glass dish. Drizzle with ¼ cup of Southern Comfort. Top with another layer of watermelon wedges and drizzle with remaining ¼ cup of Southern Comfort. Cover, refrigerate and allow watermelon to marinate for 1 hour.

- Remove marinated watermelon from refrigerator and transfer watermelon wedges to a serving platter. Drizzle with leftover marinating liquor. Don't waste the watermelon-infused Southern Comfort juices.

- Sprinkle with Sweet Spice BBQ Rub and chopped fresh mint.

- Drizzle with reserved Southern Comfort balsamic vinegar syrup.

- Serve immediately.

SERVES 4-8

GET STICKY!

World Famous BBQ from Ted's kitchen to your grill!

Ted's exciting line up of BBQ sauces & rubs include:
Beerlicious, Crazy Canuck, Pineapple Rum, Fig'N Delicious,
Orgasmic Onion & Bone Dust.

Sauces and rubs are available at Metro Grocery Stores in Ontario and
at Canadian Tire nationally.

Ted Reader's Signature Series Grills are available at Canadian Tire.

For more information & recipes visit: Tedreader.com